CUBA

Cuba Libre!

3 Manuscripts in 1 Book, Including: History of Cuba, Cuba Travel Guide and Havana Travel Guide

Carlos Fernando Alvarez

Table of Contents

HISTORY OF
CUBA

CUBA LIBRE!

Cuban History from
Christopher Columbus
to Fidel Castro

CARLOS FERNANDO ALVAREZ

BOOK 1

HISTORY OF CUBA

Cuba Libre!

Cuban History from Christopher Columbus to Fidel Castro

Carlos Fernando Alvarez

Table of Contents

Introduction

Cuba has a certain charm that may not be experienced anywhere else in the world. As a former Spanish colony, it shares numerous cultural traits with neighboring Caribbean, South American, and Central American countries. However, Cuba's history and political climate make the country a unique tourist attraction.

Cuba has a lot to offer each visitor. Tourists seeking privacy can enjoy a secluded vacation at an exclusive resort. Backpackers seeking to experience an authentic Caribbean culture may delight in the Havana neighborhoods. For those history aficionados, the colonial buildings and vintage cars would surely leave a mark.

The culture of Cuba is vibrant and varied, and its music – rumba, timba, and salsa, among other music styles – has become globally renowned. A visit to Cuba offers more than just a chance to bask in the Caribbean sun.

Before the 1950s, Cuba was a playground for European and American jetsetters. However, Cuba's alliance with the communist Soviet Union and its uneasy relationship with the United States curbed the influx of tourists for a number of years.

Since the 1990s, tourism experienced a resurgence and has become a vital part of the country's economy. Despite the country's political situation, the Cuban people maintain an openness and friendliness not usually found in other tourist destinations.

Tourists, especially those individuals interested in history, would be delighted to know more about how Cuba became the vibrant country it is today. The following chapters detail Cuba's history, from its Spanish colonial past, the country's involvement in various wars, important revolutionaries and leaders, the country's relationship with the United States, and other matters of historical significance.

Chapter 1: Pre-Spanish and Spanish Occupation

The first known residents of Cuba inhabited the island during the 4th millennium BCE. Levisa – Cuba's oldest known archaeological site – dates from around 3100 BCE. Other sites date from around 2000 BCE, most represented by western Cuba's Guayabo Blanco and Cayo Redondo cultures.

The Neolithic cultures used ground stone, shell ornaments, and tools, including the gladiolitos. The Guayabo Blanco and Cayo Redondo cultures followed a lifestyle of hunting, collecting wild plants, and fishing.

Before the arrival of Christopher Columbus, the Guanajatabey people, who had populated Cuba for centuries, were forced to vacate to the island's far west by the arrival of the Ciboney and Taino peoples, who had migrated from the South American mainland via the Caribbean island chain.

The Ciboney and Taino were part of the Arawak cultural group, who lived in South America before the Europeans' arrival. They first settled at Cuba's eastern portion before venturing out west. Bartolome de la Casas, a Spanish Dominican clergyman, estimated that the Taino people's population had reached 350,000 towards the end of the 15th century.

The Taino grew yucca, harvested the root crop, and baked it to make cassava bread. The Taino also grew tobacco and cotton, and ate sweet potatoes and maize.

In the History of the Indians, the Taino had "everything needed to live; they had many crops."

The Spanish Occupation

The arrival of Christopher Columbus in Cuba in 1492 heralded the start of Spanish occupation in the Americas. According to his journal, he had never seen anything so beautiful. Everything he saw was so lovely that his eyes could not tire of seeing such beauty; nor could he get tired of listening to the birds singing. According to him, there were thousands of tree species, with each tree bearing a unique fruit with a delicious flavor.

On the island, the Spanish prospected for gold. However, they did not know that the island's real value lay in its strategic location and rich soil. Cuba lies at the center of three major maritime routes: to the east (the Windward Passage), to the north (the Straits of Florida), and to the west (the Yucatan Channel) that enables both access to the Caribbean and the Gulf of Mexico.

At the intersection, Spain was the most vulnerable to foreign invasion. For two centuries, the country was a launching pad and home base for several important Spanish expeditions in the Americas. Cuba, which was dubbed the "Spanish fortress of the Caribbean," was touted by Spain as an important strategic colony.

The Ciboney and Taino people were the island's inhabitants when the Spaniards arrived, and they lived by farming, hunting, and fishing. Like the Puerto Rico Tainos, Cuba's Indian population was decimated by European diseases and hard labor. The Taino and

Ciboney cultivated tobacco and taught the Spaniards how to roll and smoke tobacco.

Spanish conquest in Cuba began nearly 20 years after Columbus arrived. The Cuban territory's control and conquest was handed over to Diego Velazquez, one of Hispaniola's richest landowners. The colonization process began in 1510. Warned of the Spanish activities on neighboring islands, Cuba's eastern aboriginals offered resistance against the invasion. Their leader, Hatuey, was caught and burned alive as an example.

In 1513, the village of Nuestra Señora de la Asunción de Baracoa was established. Seven other villages, with the intent of controlling the conquered lands, were created: Bayamo in 1513; Sancti Spiritus, Santisima Trinidad, and San Cristóbal de la Habana in 1514; Puerto Principe and Santiago de Cuba in 1515.

The economy of Cuba during the Spanish period was based on enslaving the native Indians, who were handed to the Spaniards via the 'encomienda' system, which was a non-transferable and revocable personal grant or concession. In the system, the colonizer must feed and clothe the natives, and teach them Christianity. The colonizer was then entitled to make the natives work for him. The encomienda system was a reason for the rapid decimation of the native Cuban population.

During the first years of colonization, the most significant economic activity was gold mining. Aside from Indians, the Spaniards also used Black slaves, who gradually integrated into the Cuban population. With the gold depleted, cattle soon turned into Cuba's main income source in the forms of leather and salted beef. At the same time, the Spaniards in Cuba started other forms of trade in the emerging Spanish empire.

Three centuries after colonization, Cuba remained an overlooked stopping point for Spain's fleet, which visited the Americas and returned to Spain with continental America's mineral wealth. During the 19th century, Cuba dramatically experienced a resurgence.

Haiti's collapse as a sugar-producing colony, the United States' rise as an independent nation, the ingenuity of the Creole business community of Cuba, and Spanish protective policies all led to the rise of a sugar revolution in Cuba. In a few years, Cuba became the world's major producer of sugar.

Slaves arrived in droves; sugar replaced agriculture, tobacco, and cattle as the primary economic source; large estates competed with smaller estates; Spain gave more attention to the Cuban economy; and prosperity replaced poverty. The last two factors helped in delaying a motion for independence early in the 19th century. Cuba remained loyal to Spain, as most other Latin American countries were cutting ties.

By the end of the 19th century, the loyalty of Cuba started to change as a result of Spaniards competing with Creoles for the island's governance. It led to the rise of Cuban nationalism and increased Spanish taxation and despotism. Such developments resulted in a war – The Ten Years' War – that still failed to gain independence for Cuba.

During the second independence war (1895 to 1898), José Marti – a major Cuban independence leader – was killed in battle. As a result of increasingly strained relations between the United States and Spain, the Americans entered the Cuban conflict in 1898.

Chapter 2: The Wars for Independence

As early as 1790, the idea for Cuban independence from Spain floated among some groups. José Antonio Aponte led the first revolutionary attempt in 1791. However, the uprising failed. While no uprisings occurred in the next few decades, the freedom ideal was not forgotten.

In 1825, Simón Bolivar heard of plans to liberate Cuba from Spain from a junta established in Mexico. Bolivar spoke of campaigning for Cuban independence, but the project was aborted as it was too complicated. The next serious attempt for independence occurred in 1850. Narcisó Lopez arrived from New York to Cuba with 600 men. While they conquered Cárdenas, the revolutionaries did not get popular support and they were forced to leave the island.

The next few years witnessed a few more failed attempts at independence. Beginning in 1855, conspirators were executed followed by a period of calm for over 10 years.

Cuban representatives, in 1866, traveled to Spain to meet with Spanish representatives in Madrid. The Cubans needed more investments to modernize sugar plants. The conversations failed, however, which prompted the Spaniards to lower customs rights. The Spaniards then learned that, for Cubans, the lowering of rights led to revolution and the wars for Cuban independence.

The Ten Years War

Also known as the Great War (1868 to 1878), the Ten Years War began on October 10, 1868 under Carlos Manuel de Céspedes. He was supported by the Sugar Mill La Demajagua patriots, and called for Cuba's independence. On October 11, 1868, Céspedes unsuccessfully attacked the village of Yara.

The Yara revolution extended throughout the entire area of Oriente of Cuba, and patriots converged in various parts of the island to support Céspedes. On February 27, 1874, Céspedes was killed in an ambush by Spanish troops. Activity in the Ten Years War came to a head in 1872 and 1873. However, military operations were limited to the regions of Oriente of Cuba and Camagüey due to a supplies shortage.

On February 8, 1878, peace negotiations started in Zanjón, Puerto Principe. Two days later, the governments of Spain and Cuba accepted the peace terms, and the Ten Years War ended, although protests by a group of Antonio Maceo followers continued. On May 28, 1878, Maceo ended the protests.

Smallest War

The Smallest War occurred from 1879 to 1880. On August 24, 1879, a new war against the Spanish authorities began in Oriente of Cuba. The war started because of the dissatisfaction of the revolutionaries during the Ten Years War, and the economic and political consequences of the previous war.

The new generals in the Smallest War included Calixto Garcia, Guillermo Moncada, José Maceo (Antonio's brother), Emilio Nuñez, and Francisco Carrillo. While the war was started enthusiastically, it did not gain enough magnitude as the rest of the country sought peace.

While the Smallest War lasted for less than a year, it indicated that the peace deals in Zanjón were not meant to last.

Independence War

The second war for independence occurred from 1895 to 1898. Unlike in the Ten Years War, the United States did not ignore the Cuban Independence Movement of the 1890s. The United States had become a different nation than it had been during 1865. Immigration to the United States was high, the Civil War was over, and people began to settle in the American West. Historian Stephen Ambrose had said the U.S. needed to "find a new outlet for its dynamic nature and energy."

Journalists like Joseph Pulitzer and William Randolph Hearst were fascinated with the Cuban struggle, and they used sensationalist, dramatic stories to sell their newspapers. Hearst and other journalists had succeeded to bring American attention to the Cuban people's suffering.

The 1895 revolution's central leaders included Calixto Garcia, Maximo Lopez, and Jose Marti. Gomez, who lived from 1836 to 1905, became the Cuban revolution's military leader. Garcia was instrumental to the U.S. military's success in Cuba. He provided vital intelligence to the U.S. military, including information on Spanish officers and maps. After his death, Marti became a revolutionary martyr.

Spain sent 100,000 soldiers to Cuba in 1895. After the U.S. intervened in 1898, Spanish rule in Cuba ended. However, Spain's defeat and the presence of the Americans in Cuba raised new issues for the island nation.

The Cruiser "Maine" Incident and the End of the War

President William McKinley, on January 24, 1898, deployed the USS Maine to Havana. On February 15, 1898, at 9:40 p.m., an accident (freak or sabotage) caused an explosion that killed 260 sailors and plunged the USS Maine to the ocean floor. The USS Maine was one of the U.S. Navy's new steam-powered, steel-hulled battleships, and was one of the largest battleships.

Three days after the explosion of the Maine, Hearst's newspaper sold over one million copies, becoming the first newspaper to do so. Hearst and Pulitzer's war slogan 'Remember the Maine' prompted the U.S. to intervene in the war.

On April 19, 1898, the United States Congress adopted the Joint Resolution for War with Spain, and, on April 25, 1898, the U.S. formally declared war. The would-be U.S. president, Teddy Roosevelt, resigned from his post at the Navy and joined the war. He financed personally his expedition and outfitted his 'Rough Riders' troops. The Rough Riders took the San Juan Hill away from the Spaniards.

The battle between the U.S. and Spanish naval forces – the Battle of Santiago Bay – ended centuries of Spanish conquest in the West. One American died, while 1,800

Spaniards perished in battle. The Spanish ships were either sinking, burning, or beached. The Spanish forces in Santiago surrendered two weeks later.

On August 11, 1898, the U.S. and Spain agreed on peace terms, in which the U.S. received four new territories: Puerto Rico, Cuba, Guam, and the Philippines. Spain was paid $20 million for Puerto Rico, the Philippines, and Guam.

Albeit the treaty recognized Cuban independence, the American (not the Cuban) flag was raised over Havana. During the Santiago de Cuba surrender ceremonies, Calixto Garcia and his fellow revolutionaries were not permitted to participate.

Chapter 3: U.S. Occupation and the Platt Amendment

After the Cuban war for independence, an American military government was proclaimed immediately in the island, with the installation of General John R. Brooke as commander. The Cuban revolutionary government was not allowed to take control.

General Brooke, on January 1, 1899, formally wrested control of Havana from the governor general. General Máximo Gómez, in a diary entry dated January 8, 1899, stated that "Cuba cannot have true moral peace, which is what people need for their good fortune and happiness...The transitional government was imposed by a foreign power by force and is illegitimate and incompatible with the principles that the country has been upholding..."

The U.S. government was backed by the Teller Amendment, which placed Cuba in a position different from previous Spanish colonies. The Brooke administration restored certain services while controlling postal services, customs, health agencies, and sanitation.

Brooke's successor, General Leonard Wood, in December 1899, started the second period of U.S. administration in Cuba. The progressive Wood led the most advanced Cuban reconstruction programs. He campaigned for the eradication of yellow fever and malaria in Cuba. Under Wood's administration, students were enrolled, schools were built, teachers were given special training, and the University of

Havana was rebuilt. Programs were also instituted for bridge, road, and railroad improvement.

In 1900, a new law was passed that allowed Cubans to elect leaders at a municipal level. A constitution was drafted, with a provision for universal suffrage, a bicameral legislature, an elected president, and a separation of church and state. The U.S. accepted the Cuban constitution as long as it would keep its upper hand in its dealings with Cuba. The additional clauses became known as the Platt Amendment.

The clauses stipulated that Cuba should not contract debts that may not be repaid by conventional revenues and that Cuba should not participate in treaties that may impair sovereignty. Moreover, Cuba should accept the legality of military government acts, allow the U.S. to buy or lease lands for naval stations or coaling, and give the U.S. privileges to intervene in the preservation of Cuban independence or to support a government that can protect individual liberties, life, and property.

The amendment seemed to restrict Cuban self-determination. While the Cuban assembly revised the amendment's terms, the U.S. turned it down. Due to the humiliation to the Cubans brought on by the amendment, debates ensued until the Platt Amendment was repealed in 1934.

Cuba, on June 12, 1901, ratified the amendment as an addendum to the 1901 Cuban constitution and the sole alternative to the U.S.'s permanent military occupation. The U.S., nevertheless, leased a naval coaling station at Guantanamo Bay until the 1980s. The rights were acquired under the May 1903 Treaty of Relations terms and the July 1903 Lease of Agreement. Even until today, the Guantanamo Bay issue remains a sore spot for many Cubans.

On May 20, 1902, the Cuban flag was raised over Havana as the country swore in its first president – Tomás Estrada Palma.

Chapter 4: Cuba's Reform Movements

Reformism in Cuba had begun even during the Spanish period. As the possibility of independence from Spain was still remote, several Cubans attempted to make reforms within the Spanish Empire. Reformismo (reformism) was a Cuban movement beginning in the 19th century that sought to reform Spanish institutions in Cuba.

Reformismo spurred in the middle of the century, partially because of the failure of numerous conspiracies aimed at expelling Spain and due to black uprisings against slavery in Cuba. At the time, Spain also seemed to adhere to a more lenient policy toward its Caribbean colony.

The 1865 reform movement was strong enough to organize the Partido Reformista (Reformist Party), the first political party to be established on the island. The party generally advocated for equal rights among Peninsulars and Cubans, limitation of the captain-general's powers, and greater political freedom in Cuba.

The reform party also advocated the gradual abolition of slavery, freer trade, and an increase of white migrants into the island. In 1865, the slave trade was partially abolished. On November 5, 1879, the Spanish governor signed a law abolishing slavery in Cuba. However, the royal decree that abolished slavery completely was enforced on October 7, 1886.

Some Peninsulars, who formed the Partido Incondicional Espanol (Unconditional Spanish Party), soon opposed the Reformists' activities. The Peninsulars used the Diario de la Marina newspaper to attack the Cuban reformers.

The reformists' work and their dispute with the Peninsulars affected Spain. After a successful independence movement in Santo Domingo against Spain in 1865, and at the time when Spain was experiencing political and economic difficulties, Spain's monarchy felt it was best to temper its Cuban policy.

The Junta de Informacion (Information Board) was soon established, and comprised of four Peninsulars and 12 Creole reformers. The Spanish government also ordered the Cuban municipalities to set high voting qualifications. As 12 Creoles were elected, it meant the Cubans were more open to reform than independence.

However, reforms within Cuba under Spain were short-lived. The Spanish government, while allowing the junta to meet, did not allow the implementation of the board's recommendations. In 1867, not only did the Spanish government disband the board, it also slapped on new taxes. The disbandment of the Junta de Informacion and of reformism gave rise to the independence movement. Creoles soon started to move for separation from Spain.

Agrarian Reforms

Cuba's agrarian reform laws sought to break up larger landholdings and give the back the lands to tenants, the state, and cooperatives. The land reform laws were first passed from 1959 to 1963, after the Cuban Revolution. The Argentinian revolutionary Che Guevara was declared the INRA's (Instituto Nacional de Reforma Agraria) minister of industries and oversaw the policies related to land reform.

Che Guevara, on January 27, 1959, declared that the Cuban government's main concern was 'the social justice that land redistribution brings about.' The Agrarian Reform Law went into effect on May 17, 1959. The law called for the limitation of farm sizes to 12 square kilometers (3,333 acres) and real estate to 4 square kilometers (1,000 acres).

Any holdings beyond the limits set by the law were taken by the government and were either held as state-run communities or redistributed to peasants in 271,139 square meters (67 acres). Foreigners may also not own sugar plantations.

For lands acquired by the government, the compensation was Cuban currency bonds to mature at 4.5% interest in 20 years. Bonds were based on assessed land values for tax purposes. American landowners during Fulgencio Batista's rule had lands assessed at low rates.

INRA had its own militia with 100,000 personnel. They were enlisted to help the government take control of the land and supervise distribution. The militia were later enlisted to help establish cooperative farms. U.S. corporations had owned most of the seized lands with a total area of 1,942 square kilometers (480,000 acres).

Che Guevara eventually trained the militia as a regular army. The INRA also funded most of the country's highway construction, and built tourist resorts and rural housing based on Guevara's industrial plans.

On October 1963, a Second Agrarian Reform Law was passed and enacted.

Chapter 5: The Cuban Republic and Revolution

President Tomás Estrada Palma's government was heavily influenced by the U.S. During the 1905 and 1906 elections, he tried to hold on to power. However, the Liberals contested the elections, which led to a rebellion and another United States occupation in September 1906.

William Howard Taft, the U.S. Secretary of War, attempted to resolve the issue but failed, and Palma eventually resigned. Charles Magoon was then appointed the provisional governor. In January 1909, Magoon handed the government over to José Miguel Gómez, the Liberal president. At the same time, Cuba steadily grew economically, and sugar prices continually rose until the 1920s.

However, Gómez's administration, which ran from 1909 to 1913, established a pattern of corruption, graft, fiscal irresponsibility, maladministration, and social insensitivity – particularly toward African-Cubans. Led by Pedro Ivonet and Evaristo Estenoz, the Afro-Cubans organized to secure more political patronage and better jobs.

Corruption continued under the administrations of Mario García Menocal (from 1913 to 1921), Alfredo Zayas (from 1921 to 1925), Gerardo Machado y Morales (from 1925 to 1933), Fulgencio Batista (from 1939 to 1944 and 1952 to 1959), Ramón Grau San Martin (from 1944 to 1048), and Carlos Prío Socarrás (from 1948 to 1952).

Machado was one of Cuba's most notorious presidents, holding on to power through assassinations, troops, and manipulation. In the Revolution of 1933, the U.S. government aided leftists to take Machado down. Batista then replaced Machado.

During the time, sugar comprised about 4/5 of the country's export earnings, and was supported by a tourist trade based on Havana's casinos, hotels, and brothels, especially during the United States' Prohibition years (1919 to 1933). As the 1950s ended, Cuba was one of Latin America's leading economies. However, rural workers earned only ¼ of the average $353 per capita annual income.

Most Cubans, especially those in the countryside, experienced poverty, unemployment, underemployment, and a lack of public services. The U.S. and other foreign investors had control of the economy, and Batista absolutely controlled the political system.

The Revolution and the Fall of Batista

The fall of Fulgencio Batista resulted from the country's internal political decay and Fidel Castro's 26th of July Movement, which remembered Castro's botched attack on the Moncada military base on July 26, 1953. Batista's fall may also have been due to opposition groups like Federation of University Students not satisfied with Batista's rule.

Castro, who was born on August 13, 1926, was a legislative candidate for the 1952 elections, which Batista aborted. Castro and a few of his friends, in 1955, departed for Mexico to prepare for the ousting of the

Cuban government. In December 1956, Castro and a group of rebels, were on board the yacht, Granma. Castro and his group landed in southeastern Cuba, where security forces routed and annihilated them.

Castro, his brother Raul, Che Guevara, and a few more survivors, fled to the Sierra Maestra and started a guerrilla campaign. In the following years, the rebel group had successfully recruited hundreds of Cuban volunteers. They also won battles against Batista's armed forces, and went to the island's west.

At the same time, communist groups and certain members of the non-communist Federation of University Students staged attacks and strikes in urban areas. The U.S., in 1958, cut off the Batista government with an arms embargo. Moreover, some military commanders of Cuba joined in or sympathized with the rebellion. Early on January 1, 1959, Batista fled the country. After he departed, around 800 Castro supporters set into Havana, having overcome a 30,000-strong army.

The Aftermath

The 26th of July Movement had relatively insignificant support, vague political plans, and untested governing skills. However, the movement rapidly forged a following among urban workers, poor peasants, idealists, and the youth. Dating to 1925, the Communist Party of Cuba assumed the country's main political role. The country then patterned itself on Eastern Europe's Soviet-bloc countries, and Cuba became the Americas' first socialist country.

Castro's new regime effectively dissolved Cuba's capitalist system by collectivizing agricultural production, setting up a centrally-planned economy, forging close economic ties with the Soviet Union, and developing various social services – especially in the rural areas.

The new regime also eradicated what's left of Batista's army and established new institutions of farmers and professional workers. The Castro regime nationalized hundreds of millions of dollars in private businesses and U.S. property. Such acts by the new regime set off the U.S. government's retaliatory measures like a trade embargo and an invasion (unsuccessful) by Cuban exiles at the Bay of Pigs in April 1961. More operations to overthrow Castro did not succeed and he went on to become one of the world's longest-ruling presidents. Batista died on August 6, 1973 in Estoril, Portugal at the age of 72.

Chapter 6: The Castro Era

The United States' antagonistic actions, however, only pushed Fidel Castro to the Soviet Union and strengthened popular support for him. In December of 1961, Castro declared that he was a communist.

The Cuban leadership and the country in general were divided over Cuba's shift to communism and the country's increasing dependence on the Soviet Union. Hundreds of thousands of Cuban investors and skilled workers defected to the United States (mainly to Miami, Florida) and other countries like Spain.

In the initial years of Fidel Castro's administration, Soviet military and economic support were crucial, and the Soviets' moves often roused strong opposition from the United States.

The October 1962 Cuban Missile Crisis was a serious incident. After the Union of Soviet Socialist Republics (U.S.S.R.) installed nuclear missile stations on the island, the world was almost at war, and the United States installed a naval blockade of Cuba and demanded the Soviets to remove the missiles.

The island country was also affected by shortages of fuel, food, and other necessities. The second agrarian reform law in 1963 ended the diversification attempts on the economy, which was still dependent of sugar cane. In 1964, Cuba renewed efforts to export revolution by meeting with Latin American communists in Havana. In 1965, Cuba almost stoked a civil war in the Dominican Republic, which prompted the United States military to intervene in Cuba's neighbor.

In Kinshasa, Congo, Che Guevara engaged in covert operations. In 1967, Guevara was killed while trying to start a revolution in Bolivia. Afterwards, many Caribbean states and Latin American countries alienated Cuba for its attempts to brew conflict.

In the late 1960s, the Cuban government restored its attacks on private property by nationalizing numerous small businesses. Officers of the military occupied high posts in industry, the government, and the Cuban Communist Party. Castro's regime sought to foster nationalism and boost production by offering moral incentives and encouraging labor organizations.

The Castro government eventually returned to Soviet-style planning and a conventional system of socialist incentives. A new constitution in 1976 and a new code for elections reorganized the country's political system. Fidel Castro became president of the Council of State and of the Council of Ministers; thus, combining effectively the roles of prime minister and president.

During the 1970s, conditions improved. Shortages and bottlenecks were significantly eliminated. Isolation from world diplomacy gained Cuba a leadership role among non-aligned nations and developing countries. Cubans offered commercial, military, and technical assistance to several states in Latin America, Africa, and the Caribbean region. Cuba, however, lost influence as it supported the 1979 Soviet invasion of Afghanistan.

In the 1980s, Cuban military assistance influenced civil wars in Ethiopia and Angola, and civilian personnel contributed to Latin America and Asia. In 1983, the U.S. invaded Grenada, killing dozens of Cubans and banishing from the island what was left of Cuba's aid force. From 1989 to 1991, Cuba slowly removed its troops from Angola.

Soviet aid to Cuba in the forms of war material, petroleum, loans, and technical advice was vital and comprised a major portion of the country's annual budget. The U.S.S.R. also bought a significant portion of Cuban sugar at generally higher prices.

Soviet-Cuban relations crumbled as Soviet economic, social, and political policies were liberalized during the late 1980s. However, the Cuban government did not modify its stance on economic and social policy.

In September 1991, Soviet troops started to withdraw its troops from Cuba over the island country's objections that withdrawing troops would compromise Cuba's security. Cuba's troubled economy, when the U.S.S.R. dissolved later in 1991, further suffered from the loss of vital economic and military support that had effectively constituted subsidies.

In the middle of internal shortages, and with dissatisfaction and unrest growing, Fidel Castro announced a 'special period in peacetime' of energy conservation, reduced public services, and food rationing. Aside from the increase in unemployment, the ongoing trade embargo by the U.S. worsened shortages of medical supplies, food shortages, fuel, and raw materials.

The government, in 1993, legalized small businesses like family restaurants (paladres), U.S. dollar use, and private employment. In 1994, independent farmers' markets and farms were encouraged. The Cuban government also attracted non-Cuban capitalists, including Spanish and Canadian hoteliers.

In 1997, Christmas again became a national holiday, in anticipation of Pope John Paul II's visit in 1998. Led by tourism, Cuba's economy significantly improved. However, Cubans were starting to doubt socialism's future.

After Cuba downed two U.S. aircraft in 1996, the U.S. Congress passed the Helms-Burton Law, which threatened to sanction foreign companies investing in Cuba. Dissidents in Cuba, in 1999, were jailed. Early in the 21st century, Cuba gained from a Venezuelan petroleum trade agreement, which eased some of Cuba's more restrictive social and economic policies.

Fidel Castro, on July 31, 2006, provisionally passed on power to his brother, Raul Castro, as the former recovered from intestinal surgery. Fidel Castro, in February 2008, stated officially that he would not accept another presidential term. The Cuban National Assembly then chose Raul as the country's next leader.

Under Raul, Cuba implemented several reforms. The country's equal pay system was abolished. Cubans are now allowed to buy personal computers and cellular phones, and can stay at hotels reserved formerly for foreigners.

In 2003, the European Union sanctioned Cuba for repression of its dissidents. The European Union lifted the sanctions in 2008, prompting criticism from the United States. In September 2010, Raul Castro announced the toleration of private enterprises and laid off around 500,000 government employees.

The National Assembly, in 2011, approved measures to free up the economy. Some of the steps include the state's reduced role in the retail, transportation, construction, and agricultural sectors, along with the encouragement of private business development.

By 2012, some estimated 390,000 Cubans had started cuenta-propistas (self-employment enterprises) including businesses like auto-repair shops, beauty parlors, restaurants, and taxi services. On February 2013, Raul Castro announced that he would not seek for reelection when his term would end in 2018.

Chapter 7: Cuba in the Cold War Era

Cuba has significantly figured in the Cold War with the Bay of Pigs Invasion and the Cuban Missile Crisis. While Cubans welcomed Castro's overthrow of Batista, Cuba's new political order made American government officials nervous. Although considered repressive and corrupt, Batista was an ally to U.S. companies and was pro-American. Batista was anti-communist and did not restrict American operations in Cuba.

Fidel Castro, on the other hand, disapproved of how Americans conducted business in Cuba. He believed it was time for Cubans to take control of their nation. One of his popular slogans was "Cuba Sí, Yanquis No."

Upon assuming power, Castro moved to reduce American influence on Cuba. He nationalized American-controlled industries like mining and sugar, called on fellow Latin American governments to be more autonomous, and announced land reform plans.

As a response, U.S. President Dwight D. Eisenhower authorized the Central Intelligence Agency (CIA) to recruit 1,400 Miami-based Cuban exiles and train them to overthrow Castro.

Castro, in May 1960, established ties with the Soviet Union, and the U.S. retaliated by banning Cuban sugar importation. To prevent the collapse of the sugar economy, the Soviet Union agreed to purchase the sugar. The U.S. government, in January 1961, cut diplomatic ties with Cuba and began preparations for an invasion.

Several State Department and other advisors to John F. Kennedy, the new American president, asserted that Castro would not be an American threat. However, Kennedy believed that orchestrating Castro's removal would show China, Russia, and skeptical Americans that he was determined to win the Cold War.

President Kennedy had inherited his predecessor's campaign to equip and train a Cuban exile guerrilla army, but he had doubts about the plan's wisdom. Officers of the CIA informed Kennedy they could keep a covert involvement in the invasion. If all goes well, the plan would spur an anti-Castro uprising on Cuba.

The plan's first part was to destroy Castro's air force. A group of Cuban exiles, on April 15, 1961 departed Nicaragua in American B-26 bombers, painted to resemble stolen Cuban planes. The exiles struck the Cuban airfields. However, Castro knew of the plan and moved his planes to a safe location.

The Cuban exile brigade, on April 17, 1961, started its invasion at an area on Cuba's southern shore – the Bay of Pigs. However, the invasion was unsuccessful. While the CIA sought secrecy on the operation, a radio station had broadcast every detail of the operation all over Cuba. Furthermore, backup paratroopers set foot in the wrong area.

Not long after, Castro's troops caught the beach invaders, and the exiles surrendered in less than one day. Over 1,100 were taken prisoner and 114 were killed. Another diplomatic misfire, the 1962 Cuban missile crisis, further fanned American-Cuban-Soviet tensions.

The Cuban Missile Crisis

On October 1962, leaders of the United States and the Soviet Union, during the Cuban Missile Crisis, engaged in a 13-day military and political standoff over the installation of Soviet missiles (nuclear-armed) in Cuba.

In an October 22, 1962 television address, President Kennedy informed the Americans about the missiles' presence, explained why he enacted a naval blockade surrounding Cuba, and made clear the U.S. was ready to forcefully neutralize the national security threat.

A crucial Cuban missile crisis event occurred on October 24, 1962, when Cuba-bound Soviet ships approached the group of U.S. vessels enforcing the blockade. A Soviet attempt to breach the blockade could have likely sparked a confrontation and an eventual nuclear exchange. However, the Soviets did not breach the blockade.

The standoff between the U.S. and the Soviet Union continued. On October 27, 1962, an American reconnaissance plane was brought down over the island, and an invasion force was being prepared in Florida.

While many people on both sides feared the crisis would have led to World War III, the American and Soviet leaders found a way out of the situation. Meanwhile, the Soviets and Americans had communicated with one another. On October 26, 1962, Khrushchev informed Kennedy, offering to remove missiles from Cuba in exchange for a promise from American leaders not to invade Cuba.

The next day, Khrushchev proposed to the U.S. that the U.S.S.R. would take away its missiles in Cuba if the

Americans removed their Turkey missile installations. The Kennedy administration officially decided to comply with the first message's terms and ignore entirely Khrushchev's second letter. In private, however, the U.S. agreed to withdraw the U.S. missiles in Turkey.

Robert Kennedy, the U.S. attorney general at the time, delivered in person the message to the Soviet ambassador in Washington. On October 28, 1962, the Cuban Missile Crisis ended.

The Cuban Missile Crisis had a sobering effect on both the Soviets and Americans. In 1963, a direct communication link was established between Moscow and Washington to help defuse further diplomatic situations, and the two world powers signed treaties related to nuclear artillery.

Chapter 8: Cuba-U.S. Relations and the Trade Embargo

The relationship of Cuba and the United States began when the latter started to intervene in Cuba's wars for independence against Spain. While the U.S. helped Cuba achieve independence, and even briefly colonized Cuba until 1902, the military of the U.S. continued to intervene in Cuba's affairs until 1934. The U.S. also continued to dominate trade within Cuba until 1953.

Below are some of the highlights of Cuban relations with the United States.

In 1953, Fidel Castro, who was a lawyer, led the revolution against Fulgencio Batista. The U.S. sold arms to Batista, who was their ally, even if he resisted calls to step down or reform. Around 1958, Batista began to be defeated by Castro. The U.S. subsequently denied asylum to Batista, who eventually settled in Portugal.

In April 1959, Castro accepted an invitation from U.S. newspapers to visit New York, where he visited the Bronx Zoo and Yankee Stadium, spoke before the Council of Foreign Affairs, and met editors. Instead of meeting U.S. President Dwight Eisenhower, Castro met Richard Nixon, U.S.'s then-vice president, and Dean Acheson, the secretary of state.

In April 1961, the botched Bay of Pigs invasion was carried out. Shortly after, on October 1962, Cuba got embroiled in the U.S.-Soviet Union conflict in a historical event that was known as the Cuban Missile Crisis.

A few decades later, on April 1980, the Mariel Boatlift event occurred. The event was a mass emigration of Cubans, who traveled from Cuba to the U.S. between April 15, 1980 and October 31, 1980. Due to decades of economic sluggishness in Cuba, numerous Cubans swarmed Havana's Peruvian embassy after an escape attempt there left the compound unprotected.

Castro gave in to pressure and opened the doors for migration to the United States. However, he wavered on transport. The Cuban exiles in Florida amassed a fleet of 1,700 boats. By May 1980, over 100,000 Cubans landed on Florida, in which the activity overwhelmed the U.S. coast guard. Eventually, the Castro regime and U.S. President Jimmy Carter agreed mutually to end the exodus.

In November 2001, there was a slight break in the United States' trade embargo against Cuba. After Hurricane Michelle, four American food companies, including Riceland Foods and Cargill, were allowed to sell food to Cuba. Castro did not accept the offer of Washington to send humanitarian aid via non-government organizations (NGOs). However, he said he was prepared, "to acquire certain quantities of medicine and food from the United States, paying them in cash."

The years from October 2003 to December 2009 were a period of tension and change. After a tension-filled decade, including the 2000 custody battle of Elian Gonzalez and the 1996 downing of two American planes by Cuba, President George W. Bush tightened the United States' sanctions on Cuba.

Recovering from intestinal surgery, Fidel Castro, in 2006, transferred power to his brother Raul Castro. Furthermore, a delegation from the U.S. comprised of

Democrats and Republicans from Congress visit Cuba; however, they were not able to meet Raul Castro.

U.S. President Barack Obama, in 2009, eased money transfers and travel for Cuban families split between the two nations. Meanwhile, Alan Gross – an American – was imprisoned and accused of spying in Cuba.

In December 2013, a handshake between Obama and Raul Castro at a memorial for Nelson Mandela offered hope for improved U.S.-Cuban relations. In December 2014, a reconciliation between the papacy and Cuba was brokered. Senior officials in Havana and Washington made tentative steps for peace. Furthermore, Pope Francis (the first Latin American pope) sent letters personally to Raul Castro and Obama, urging reconciliation.

Canada and the Vatican also hosted diplomatic meetings. Over a period of 18 months, Havana and Washington agreed to slowly thaw diplomatic relations. In December of 2014, Raul Castro and Obama stated they would normalize diplomatic relations – despite the Congress-mandated trade embargo. Moreover, Raul Castro and Obama also agreed to free Alan Gross and three Cubans for spying.

In a speech, Raul Castro emphasized the need to remove U.S. commercial, financial, and economic blockade of Cuba. The embargo, which was codified by U.S. law, was subject to the U.S. Congress's action and beyond the scope of the executive authority of President Obama.

The Embargo

When Fidel Castro assumed power in 1959, most of the Cuban economy was under the control of American corporations. The industries controlled by U.S. firms included railroads and utilities. The American firms also controlled a huge portion of Cuba's natural resources like cattle, sugar, timber, tobacco, mining, oil, and most of the nation's farmland.

Castro's government nationalized the U.S. assets, and claimed them in the name of the Cuban citizens. The U.S. then made a series of retaliatory attacks. One of them was the trade embargo, which was an effort to topple Castro's government. After over half a century, which saw the Soviet Union breakup, the Cold War's end, and the transfer of power from Fidel Castro to Raul Castro, it is apparent that the trade embargo did not succeed.

Many argue today that the embargo has no real purpose. For them, ending the embargo will make consumers in the U.S. happy. Ending it will also boost the U.S. economy and bring a certain level of economic freedom to Cuba.

Not only has the trade of U.S. goods to Cuba been halted, but also a large degree of travel and tourism. In 1960, the initial trade restrictions on Cuba were implemented under U.S. President Eisenhower's time. The U.S. placed exports to Cuba under validated license controls, with the exception of non-subsidized medicines, medical supplies, and food. However, the action did not include travel restrictions.

President Kennedy, on February 1962, imposed the trade embargo due to Cuba's ties with the Soviet Union. On July 9, 1963, the U.S. Department of the Treasury's

OFAC (Office of Foreign Assets) issued the Cuban Assets Control Regulations that banned travel by restricting any transactions with the communist island nation.

In March 1977, the Carter administration announced the lifting of travel restrictions to Cuba from the U.S., wherein such restrictions have been implemented since the 1960s. Carter issued a travel-related transaction license for Americans visiting Cuba. Also allowed were direct flights from the U.S. mainland to Cuba.

In April 1982, President Ronald Reagan's administration re-imposed Cuba travel restrictions. However, several travel categories were allowed, including travel by filmmaking or news organization employees, U.S. government officials, persons visiting close relatives, or persons doing professional research. It did not allow ordinary business or tourist travel.

On May 13, 1999, the OFAC issued changes to the embargo regulations, which loosened restrictions on travel categories, and allowing travel for people-to-people educational exchange travel. In 2000, the OFAC granted the first specific license for such kind of travel.

On March 24, 2003, travel regulations to Cuba were amended and eliminated the people-to-people exchange licenses. On April 13, 2009, U.S. President Obama directed loosened restrictions on financial remittances and family travel. Obama's administration also widened the scope of eligible donations with gift parcels. The administration also increased links to telecommunications with Cuba.

On January 14, 2011, Obama announced that changes be made to certain policies and regulations. The measures were meant to: support Cuba's civil society, increase people-to-people contact, enhance the flow of information among Cubans, and help to promote Cubans' information independence from government authorities.

On January 16, 2015, new regulations concerning travel to Cuba are drafted. Americans can now easily travel to Cuba. In 2016, commercial flights from the U.S. mainland to Cuba are offered.

Chapter 9: The History of Havana

As the capital of Cuba, the history of Havana is much more diverse and turbulent than the rest of the country. On August 25, 2015, Diego Velázquez de Cuéllar established Havana on the island's southern coast – on the Mayabeque River banks. A 1514 map of Cuba sets the town at the mouth of the Mayabeque River.

Havana's present location was established in 1519, on a site called Puerto de Carenas ('Careening Bay'). Pánfilo de Narváez gave Havana the name San Cristóbal de la Habana. Havana started as a trading port, and was regularly attacked by pirates, French corsairs, and buccaneers. The attacks prompted the Spanish Crown to fund the main cities' first fortresses.

Ships from around the New World transported products to Havana, in order for them to be taken to Spain. The multitude of ships also fueled Havana's manufacturing and agriculture. King Philip II of Spain, on December 20, 1592, declared Havana a city.

During the 17th century, Havana expanded with the construction of buildings made out of wood. Such buildings combined Canarian characteristics and Iberian architecture styles. In 1649, a third of Havana's population was struck by an epidemic from Cartagena, Colombia. By 1740, Havana had become the Spanish Empire's only New World dry dock.

The British captured Havana during the Seven Years War beginning on June 6, 1762. Upon conquering Havana, the British established trade with their Caribbean and North American colonies. Less than one year after Havana was captured, the Peace of Paris was signed; thus, ending the war. The treaty handed over Florida to Britain in exchange for returning Havana to Spain.

After Spain regained control of the city, Havana was transformed into one of the Americas' heavily-fortified cities. On January 15, 1796, Christopher Columbus's remains were brought to Cuba from Santo Domingo. His remains rested in Havana until 1898.

During the early 19th century, trade between North America and the Caribbean flourished, and Havana thrived. Prosperity among the population led to the construction of new mansions, and Havana was considered the Paris of the Antilles.

The first railroad was built in 1837 and it was used to transport sugar to the Havana harbor. Slavery was legal in Cuba until the 1880s. After the Confederates were defeated in 1865 during the Civil War, former slaveholders in the U.S. moved to Havana and continued their operations. The city's walls were dismantled in 1863 to pave way for the metropolis's expansion.

After the War for Independence

Like in the rest of Cuba, Havana was also occupied by the United States during the turn of the 20th century. The occupation ended officially on May 20, 1902, when Tomás Estrada Palma took office as Cuba's first president.

During the Republican Period, which lasted from 1902 to 1959, Havana and the rest of Cuba experienced a boost in the economy. During the 1930s, casinos, luxury hotels, and nightclubs were built to serve the city's growing tourism industry. During the time, Havana also hosted numerous activities like musical shows, parks, Grand Prix car racing, and marinas. Around 300,000 Americans visited Havana in 1958.

After the 1959 revolution, Castro's new regime promised to improve public housing, official buildings, and social services. From May of 1959 onwards, Castro appropriated all private industry and property under a communist model supported by the Soviet Union after the trade embargo by the United States. Havana was especially hit hard by the shortages.

After the Soviet Union's decline in 1991, the Soviet subsidies stopped. Despite the political upheavals in Europe after the fall of the Soviet Union and the emergence of new countries, Havana still continued to have a communist government throughout the 1990s.

Havana is currently being renovated. After decades of prohibition, the government turned to tourism for a new revenue stream. Foreign investors are now allowed to develop the hospitality industry and construct new hotels. Old Havana has also undergone rehabilitation, with the revitalization of public squares and streets. However, revitalization efforts are concentrated in less than 10% of Old Havana's land area due to the city's large size.

Conclusion

The death of Fidel Castro on November 25, 2016 ushered in a new era for Cuba. However, change had begun when the older Castro – due to a serious illness in 2006 – handed power in 2008 to his younger brother, Raul.

Under his rule, Raul Castro moved to adjust Cuba's state-controlled system that was meant to salvage the Cuban Revolution's gains while veering its economy away from heavy reliance on Chinese largesse and Venezuelan subsidies. Under Raul, Cuba accepted new foreign investment and recovered diplomacy with the United States.

The U.S.-Cuba normalization process, which culminated in U.S. President Barack Obama's March 2016 visit, has promoted better ties to benefit both countries. However, Raul's Cuban socialism 'updating' has been limited, due in part to Fidel's shadow and his followers and their opposition to Washington, the U.S. embargo, and the Cuban exiles in Miami.

The U.S. has affected Cuba in many ways, and imperialists throughout Cuba's history have negatively and positively changed the country. Cuba is country with a brutal past and a shaky present.

Despite the country's economic and political situation, the Cuban culture still is a draw for many a tourist. As the country's main income stream, tourism is also being updated to offer more to local and foreign visitors. Cuba's future is bright, though, as the country is opening up its doors to other countries once again.

CUBA
TRAVEL GUIDE
CUBA LIBRE!

Let the Cultural History of Cuba
Guide You Through the Authentic
Soul of the Country

CARLOS FERNANDO ALVAREZ

BOOK 2

CUBA TRAVEL GUIDE

Cuba Libre!

Let the Cultural History of Cuba Guide You Through the Authentic Soul of the Country

Carlos Fernando Alvarez

Table of Contents

Introduction

Now that you have booked that long deserved holiday to Cuba, it's time for you to learn about the many interesting places to see, things to do, and places to explore in this country. You have to admit that it is indeed a beautiful country albeit with an intriguing past.

The country has actually been a popular travel destination for many foreign tourists. They have been visiting this tropical country for years. It's one of the countries in the Caribbean that have only been recently in the American tourist radar, but yeah, tourists from other countries have been frequenting the place for decades. That is due in part to an economic embargo.

Visiting Cuba is like going through a time warp. You will find a lot of the old school buildings still up and running, the beaches are absolutely great, and you'll find a lot of antique 1950s cars. It's like everyone here is stuck in that decade – the 50s I mean.

You can walk through the bustling streets and meet the lively people first hand. Another popular thing to do here is hiking up the mountains. One important thing though is to learn all there is to know about tobacco – yes, they make some of the best cigars in the world here.

Traveling to Cuba can be confusing – and downright challenging to a lot of folks – that is why this guide was put up. In these pages you'll learn about the great places to visit, where to stay (and where to sleep cheap!), where to go out, fun things to do, how to stay safe, money matters in Cuba, where (and what) to eat in this Caribbean country, and pretty much all the other fun stuff like diving and all the other things. Yes, traveling to Cuba can be pretty expensive too – so we'll include a few tips so you can travel and reduce costs along the way.

This book is designed for the absolute first time visitor in Cuba. Everything is laid out in an easy to understand manner – and everything will be in English though I do recommend that you at least learn a few common phrases in the country's local dialect before you rush on to you Cuban Adventure.

May you have a good time while exploring the Caribbean's!

Chapter 1: Getting There

Surprise, surprise, the citizens of the world have been visiting and enjoying the sites and sounds in Cuba for decades. Unfortunately, it is the American citizens who have to walk the gauntlet. Americans have practically been banned from traveling to the country for more than 50 years!

So, does it look like things are finally changing? At the time of this writing, it looks like President Trump isn't keen on allowing Americans to travel freely to Cuba. However, he also isn't making it impossible for the average Joe to get there. Note that as of 2016 some American airlines are now allowed to fly to Cuba – hurray!

The Trouble with Getting to Cuba

Okay, so if you're not an American then you won't have any problems getting to Cuba. All you need to do is to follow the usual procedures. You basically won't get any hassles getting into the country. For instance, our British friends can get a Cuba Tourist Card courtesy of their airline, and everything else pretty much goes smoothly. But if you're an American, then you have a thing or two coming.

So, how did all of the trouble start? Well, if you read the first book in this series, you will learn that something happened back in 1960. A trade embargo was imposed by the United States against this Caribbean country. Why you ask? The answer is that Cuba nationalized all the American owned oil refineries in the country. They did that without compensating the US businessmen who invested there.

Part of that embargo is a travel restriction for American citizens. In other words, technically, it is illegal to travel to Cuba, spend money there, or even to receive gifts. In simple terms, the embargo prevented all American citizens from having any transactions with the country or its citizens.

The effect of course is that the Americans have never considered Cuba as a travel destination for 5 decades. Air travel with any airline in the US going to Cuba is near impossible. On top of that, even if you did make it to the country, your credit cards and debit cards won't work there. That means if you really want to visit the country you need to bring cold hard cash – lots of it. If you run out while you're there you're in a heap of trouble.

So How Do You Get There?

The good news is that things are changing – well, it's been 50 long years since the embargo and we've had a lot of administrations come and go since then. You can still travel to Cuba but you will need to get a Cuban tourist card. Well, technically you can't travel there just as a tourist. Your trip there should be classified as one of the 12 authorized travel categories, which are the following:

- Export transactions that can be considered for authorization
- Transmission of information materials, information, imports, and exports

- Educational institute, research, or private foundation activities
- Humanitarian projects
- Support for the people of Cuba
- Workshops, clinics, public performances, athletic competitions, and exhibitions
- Religious activities
- Educational activities
- Professional meetings or professional research
- Journalistic activity
- Official US government business
- Family visits

According to the latest update (as of November 2017), according to President Trump, Americans who want to visit Cuba can no longer use the people to people tour category. It used to be a popular option since you can say that you are going on an educational tour to experience the local Cuban culture, collaborate with local artists, arrange a local community project, volunteer with a local school etc.

Nowadays you have 3 options to get to Cuba, which include the following:

1. Via special license – please refer to the list above. This license is that Cuban tourist card, which is something like a travel visa. If you want to find out about the rules that govern its use please visit the State Department's website, which you can find here:

   https://travel.state.gov/content/passports/en/country/cuba.html

2. Option number two is to travel through foreign gateway cities. Now, some people might call this illegal but it is practically another legal loophole that you can take advantage of. Here's how some people do it – they fly either to Mexico first or Canada and then they fly to Cuba from either of these two countries. TIP: you go to either Cancun in Mexico or Toronto in Canada and then book a trip (flight or bus) to Cuba.

3. Use option number one above and then fly direct from the US to Cuba. Check out the list of flight carriers below.

Understanding the Rules for Independent Travel

Now, before you jump for joy you must understand the rules. As of November 2017 Americans must travel in organized tour groups if they want to visit Cuba. If you want to travel by yourself then declare that you are going to the country under the category of "support for the Cuban people."

You declare this whenever you book flights, for lodging purposes (sometimes the Cuban folks don't really care and they won't ask, and during re-entry into the US (which also may not be asked – sometimes they won't even look at your stamps).

Tip: stay at casas particulares, support local businesses, and eat at local restaurants. Of course, if you have cash to burn then pick a hotel (there's lots of them in the tourist hotspots and main cities). Note that there are hotels that are banned by the US government

– stay away from those. The list of banned hotels is always changing so check it out from time to time – you'll find the list of banned Cuban hotels here:

https://www.state.gov/e/eb/tfs/spi/cuba/cubarestric tedlist/275331.htm

Note that the list is courtesy of the US State Department.

Flying US to Cuba

The visa process flying to Cuba from the US can be different for each airline. Note that you need to buy a Cuban tourist visa, which you can get at the airport at the check in counter. So how much is the visa? It's anywhere from $50 to a little over $100 – again, it's different for each airline. Note the following:

- Frontier – Cost is around $100+ but you must buy the visa online and then they send it via mail.
- American Airlines – around $85, buy it online too.
- United Airlines – Cuban tourist visa around $75 give or take a few and you must buy it at the gate.
- Delta – around $50 and you can purchase it at the gate
- JetBlue – also around $50 and purchased at the gate
- Southwest Air – also $50 but you have to buy the visa online

TIP: call your airline in advance just to make sure – airline policies change too you know.

The Immigration Process

What happens when you get to Cuba? The process at the immigration counter is really very simple. The officer will ask what your business is in the country and you tell them that you're there for tourism. The officer will then stamp your visa (not the passport!).

What does that tell you? Cuba wants American tourists – they always have. They don't stamp your passport because they don't want you to get in trouble when you go back to the United States.

Chapter 2: Money Matters

Now we're done with the tough matters for our US friends – I know it sucks but just like you, I also hope that times will change and the US-Cuban relations will improve soon. Like come on man, it's been half a century; can't we just get along?

Well, anyway, there's this other important matter when you are planning a trip to lovely Cuba – money matters! As stated early in this book American credit cards don't work in Cuba. That means you will need a lot of cash on hand – well, maybe not a truck load but you should bring more than enough.

Should I Bring My ATM to Cuba?

If credit cards and even debit cards don't work in Cuba that also means your ATM won't work there too – if you're an American that is. US bank cards just won't work in Cuba at the moment. The best way to go is to plan everything ahead and estimate how much you're going to spend on your trip and bring lots of cash. You can bring your ATM but you will use it outside of Cuba, like maybe when you get to Mexico or Canada. Once in Cuba, your ATM is useless as a source of cash.

Cuban Currencies

Okay, so you need to bring lots of cash, how much cash are going to get for the amount of money you're bringing. Now here's the tricky thing – there are two currencies in Cuba. Hot dang! One currency is for the locals and it's called the Cuban Peso (or CUP for short) and the other one is called the Cuban Convertible Peso (or CUC for short). The CUC is for tourists – that means they have a huge emphasis on tourism in the country. Note that the CUC is pegged to the US dollar.

That means 1 CUC is equal to 1 USD. And that also means 1 CUC is equal to 24 CUP. The local Cuban Peso is a lot less than the Cuban Convertible Peso.

BIG TIP: *DON'T EXCHANGE YOUR US DOLLARS for CUC when you arrive at the airport*. They will charge you a 10% penalty for using American dollars. That 10% penalty slash charge is on top of the other charges you will be incurring when you convert your dollars into the local currency.

Here's what you should do instead: Exchange your US dollars for British Pounds, Euros, Mexican pesos, Canadian dollars, or whatever before you exchange it for Cuban Convertible Peso. Check the exchange rates before converting your cash. Obviously, you should exchange your CUC back to US dollars at the airport before flying back to the United States.

Here's another tip that can get you more money for every dollar – withdraw your money either in Mexico or Canada. That is actually your cheapest option. Another option, but it won't be as cheap is to buy your pesos, Canadian dollars, or Euros in the United States beforehand and then exchanging them when you get to Cuba.

NOTE: there are talks about doing away with the 10% penalty for exchanging US dollars in Cuba but everything has stalled – we'll just have to wait for updates in future. You can read more about that here:

http://www.miamiherald.com/news/nation-world/world/americas/cuba/article66775447.html

Changing Your Money into the Local Currency

Here's the thing, whenever you exchange your dollars (or whatever the currency is in your country) to the local currency (i.e. CUC) then you will pay a small premium to the business that is providing you with the service. How much that premium is will vary from one service provider to the other. It also depends on the method you are using. Here are some of your options in case you need to change your money to the local currency from the cheapest method to the worst.

1. *Fellow travelers leaving Cuba and going home* – this is by far the cheapest way to exchange your dollars to CUC. Well, your fellow tourists won't need the CUC but you do. Of course, they won't be able to use the CUC when they go home. Offer to exchange currencies with them – work out the math since it's really simple: 1 USD = 24 CUC (you may want to check out current exchange rates by the way). There are no fees to pay since you're just trading currencies with one another – unless of course the other fella is trying to stiff you. The only downside is if you or the other guy can't provide exact change. You may find that you will be doing this a lot when you're in Cuba especially when you arrive or when you depart and go home.

2. **Currency exchange booths** – the currency exchange booths in Cuba are the worst. Well, I guess all currency exchange booths anywhere on planet earth is bad. You will always find these booths in airports, bus terminals, malls, and other tourist hotspots. Needless to say the rates they offer are really terrible. On top of the bad rates, they also charge a commission; it's always tacked into every transaction. Sometimes currency exchange booths are all you have going for you while in Cuba.

3. **Money Changers** – If you think currency exchange booths are bad, money changers are the worst. You can even find these guys on international borders. The worst of these guys are just plain scammers. Whenever dealing with these guys make sure to count your money twice just to make sure. You should also know the current exchange rate – good thing there's an app for that. You can get the currency app or some other currency exchange app on iTunes, Google Play, or any App Store (Amazon also has their own App Store too you know).

So, How Much Cash Should I Bring?

Well, that depends on how you will be booking your stay (hotels vs. casas etc.) and the mode of transport you will be taking. If you are backpacking and will be a bit modest in your expenses then bring at least $1,000. Bring more if you plan to book a hotel or rent a car –

car rentals are expensive in Cuba – we'll go over that in a short while.

Chapter 3: That Thing about Accommodations

One of the first things that you need to be thinking about when you travel to Cuba is to find a good place to lay your head. Of course there are lots of fancy resorts and hotels in the country's popular cities like Varadero, Trinidad, and Havana. However, as a fair warning – these hotels are not cheap.

Casas Particulares

As a cheaper alternative, you can stay in what is called a casa particular. It's a homestay or maybe you may have heard of them as a kind of guest house. There is a system here in Cuba where locals are allowed to rent part of their homes to tourists. They usually rent out their extra rooms. They will have to register with the government and they pay special taxes and fees for doing so. It's a little thing they can do on the side so they can earn extra for their families.

That means you can sample the local hospitality – sometimes the accommodations include home cooked meals. You get to experience Cuban life firsthand and sample genuine Cuban cuisine. If you're really into immersing yourself in the experience then this is the best way to go. Besides, this is actually the cheapest option while you're in the country.

How Do You Find Casas Particulares

The downside is that casas particulares usually don't have websites. Well, their owners usually don't advertise on the internet – the internet here isn't the best in the world and the country is still one of the least connected on earth. So how do you find them?

One option is to simply walk around – yes walk around. You sometimes need to ask around town. However, don't be surprised if a lot of people approach you offering you pretty anything a tourist would want. They will ask if you need help while others will sell you cigars!

However, you will most likely be approached by a jineteros – someone who knows a casa owner. He will refer one to you and even take you there himself. Of course, if he does that he gets a commission from the casa owner. It's a complete win/win for all three parties involved.

If you arrive at the airport there will be folks who will also recommend casas to you. Some will even bring pictures of the place. If you meet other tourists who just went to the place you plan on going to, then you can ask them where they stayed. In case the casa particular you go to is already fully booked, the owner will happily point you to another who is available – it's usually a friend of theirs or a neighbor.

You get the same treatment when you arrive by bus in the next town. You'll find people offering to rent their place to you. If you move out of a casa, the owner will recommend another casa in the next town where you're heading to. There are networks of casa owners so you should never run out of places to stay in.

Are Casas Particulares Even Legal?

Yes, they are 100% legal. As stated earlier, these homes need to be registered with the Cuban government. Renting a part of your home or your entire home to a tourist may sound like a strange thing to you but this is the norm in Cuba. Every registered casa will have an upside down anchor sign outside – that's how people know it's a casa; well, every government registered casa will have one.

On top of that, as stated earlier, the owner will have to pay special taxes to the government. You will also get a receipt for your stay. The owner will also take note of your passport number and put it on record. They will also need to fill out a tax record book. It's really like running a business and using your own property as your means of income. So, yeah, they are absolutely legal.

What's the Nightly Rate?

Think of casas particulares as the Cuban B&B. How much will the family charge you? It will be about $10 up to $30 a night, which isn't bad. And for that you are getting a double room. You get to interact with these wonderful people and you can ask them where to go to find the best deals too in case you want to buy food, go shopping, or hunt for souvenirs.

Does that include dinner? Not really – they rarely serve dinner so you better find a local restaurant where you can get some solid eats. However, a lot of these casas offer breakfast for a price – around 2 to 4 CUC, which isn't really a bad deal. Some meals will even be customized by the owner to your liking.

Is there a way to reduce the cost? Yes but you need to practice your haggling skills. If the owner won't budge on his price point then move on to another who may offer a cheaper price. Note that there is usually a lot of casas in town.

So, What are These Casas Like?

It's different every single time. Some of them will be setup like dorms others will be more homey coz it's the owner's home. Some casa owners will rent out an entire home where you can have some more privacy. However, don't expect to get the same deal each and every time, you're renting local homes so don't always expect things to be superb.

However, expect rooms to be kept clean. Some will have air conditioning while others will just have fans. These are businesses so expect the owners to keep their accommodations attractive and comfy since they will want to get more customers throughout the year.

What If I Want to Stay in a Hotel?

There aren't that many hostels in Cuba but there are lots of fancy hotels and resorts. If you brought enough money to splurge then here are our recommendations below. Mid-range hotels will cost you some $90 to $150 a night. Staying in a fancy hotel on the other hand will cost you somewhere from $200 to $400 a night.

Hotel Cayo Levisa

- *Address:* Palma Rubia, La Palma, Pinar del Río, Cuba
- *Best for:* diving, snorkeling, and beaches
- *Number of rooms:* 56
- *Distance from Airport:* 160 km (Havana)

This hotel is located on a small island north of Pinar del Rio. It is great for a beach or island getaway as well as diving since it has an international diving center. You get to choose from 56 different bungalows each with its own regal views of the beach and ocean. Hotel reservation is inclusive of boat transfers.

Hotel Los Jazmines

- *Address:* Carretera de Viñales km. 25. Pinar del Río, Vinales, Pinar del Río, Cuba
- *Number of rooms:* 78
- *Meal plan:* room and breakfast

This hotel is only two kilometers away from the village of Viñales. The place looks more like a Mediterranean manor with a three story building painted in pink and topped with tiles for a roof. There is a busy pool area, which often becomes busy during the day. Along the way to the pool are 16 cabanas – tropical cabin suites.

Hotel Palacio Azul

- *Address*: Calle 37 e/ 12 y 16, Cienfuegos, Cienfuegos, Cuba
- *Distance from Airport*: 10 kilometers

- *Distance from city*: 3 kilometers
- *Number of rooms:* 7

This hotel has often been described as one of the best hotels in Cienfuegos. It's a short drive to the city center and it is ideally situated. The building itself was designed by famous Italian architect Alfredo Fontana.

Hotel Iberostar Parque Central

- *Address*: Neptuno e/ Prado y Zulueta, Habana Vieja, Ciudad de la Habana, Old Havana, Havana, Cuba
- *Distance to city center*: 0 km
- *Number of Rooms*: 427
- *Distance to Airport*: 30 km

This hotel is ideally located in Havana within Central Park. It combines old colonial styles with 21st century chic interiors and architecture. Note that this is actually a 5 star hotel. It is right in the heart of the densely populated area of the city and the surrounding area is culturally vibrant. That means you can find a lot of the points of interest and attractions nearby.

Hotel Moka

- *Address*: Km 52 ½ Autopista a Pinar del Río,Comunidad Las Terrazas, Candelaria, Pinar del Río, Las Terrazas, Pinar del Rio, Cuba
- *Number of Rooms*: 42
- *Distance from city* center: 73 kilometers

- This is actually the country's first ecotourism project
- Environmentally friendly
- *Distance to Airport*: 80 KM

This is actually one of the country's most unique hotels. It features a multi-tier atrium style lobby. It is actually built around an old big lime tree. Red bark trees and other foliage line the hotel's living spaces. One of the nearby attractions is Complejo Turístico Las Terrazas.

Hotel San Basilio, Santiago de Cuba City, Cuba

- *Address*: Calle San Basilio No 403 e/ Calvario y Carnicería, Santiago de Cuba, Cuba
- *Number of Rooms*: 8
- *Distance to city center*: 0 km. -- it's right in the heart of Santiago de Cuba City
- *Distance to Airport*: 10 kilometers

If you are looking for a hotel near historic attractions then this is a pretty good choice. It is right next to the popular Parque Céspedes. If you're a fan of old architecture (this one features the best of the 1920s), then this is the place to be.

Chapter 4: Transportation Options

The next biggest issue (should I dare say problem?) in Cuba is transportation. The main transport option in the country is the state run bus system called Viazul. You can visit their official website here:

http://www.viazul.com/

The good news is that Viazul bus routes cover the entire country.

Viazul Bus Company

Fares start at $10 USD one way – of course the amount of the fare will increase depending on your destination. You can use the drop downs on the site to indicate your point of origin and your destination and the amount of the fare you need to pay will be displayed there. Unfortunately you can't book a trip online just yet (maybe they're still figuring a way to do that) though you can make reservations.

To make a reservation you need to sign up for an account on the site. Make your reservations online and then you have to be there on the day of your trip at the bus terminal or bus station and pay for your fare in person.

They have bus stations in major cities and tourist destinations. Here are their addresses and contact details:

La Habana Station

- Address: Ave. 26 y Zoológico, Nuevo Vedado. Ciudad de la Habana
- Phone: 53 (7)8836092

Pinar Del Rio Station

- Address: Juan Gualberto Gómez No. 14
- Phone: 53 (082) 75 0887

Viñales Station

- Salvador Cisnero No. 63
- Phone: 53 (08) 793195

Matanzas Station

- Address: Terminal de Ferrocarriles
- Phone: 53 (045) 291473

Varadero Station

- Address: Calle 36 y Autopista
- Phone: 53 (045)614886

Santa Clara Station

- Address: Carretera Central km 383 Esquina Oquendo
- Phone: 042 222524

Cienfuegos Station

- Address: Calle 47 s/n e/ 56 y 58
- Phone: 043 518114

Trinidad Station

- Address: Piro Guinar No. 224
- Phone: 53 (41) 992214

Sancti Spiritus Station

- Address: Carretera Central km 388 Esq. B, Maso
- Phone: 041 334983

Ciego De Avila Station

- Address: Carretera Central Extremo Este
- Phone: 53 (033) 033 203086

Camaguey Station

- Address: Carretera Central s/n esq. Perú
- Phone: 53 (032) 270396

Las Tunas Station

- Address: Francisco Varona No. 240
- Phone:53 (031) 374295

Holguin Station

- Carretera Central No. 19 e/ 20 de Mayo e Independencia
- Telf. 53 (024) 426822

Bayamo Station

- Carretera Central No. 501 Vía Santiago de Cuba
- Phone: 53 (023) 421438

Santiago De Cuba Station

- Address: Avenida Jesus Menendez esquina Paseo Marti
- Phone: 53 (022) 628484

Guantanamo Station

- Address: Carretera Central y José Martí
- Phone: 53 (021) 323713

Baracoa Station

- Address: Carretera Central y Final
- Phone: 53 (021) 641550

NOTE: routes to popular destinations in Cuba sell out really fast.

PRO TIP: Make it a habit to plan your trips ahead and buy your tickets the day before your actual trip.

Rent a Car

We all know that Cuba is famous for its old school 1950s cars. You will find that a lot of them are maintained though the level of maintenance will vary from one car rental to the other. Fair warning – renting a car (modern or vintage) will cost you some money. It's never cheap in Cuba. On top of that, there is usually more people who want to rent cars than there are cars that you can rent. With such a high demand, finding one will be like haggling for fish in a market full of cats.

Of course, renting a car has its conveniences and it's a smoother way to travel. You can rent your car for several days on end. So how much would it cost? Around $70 to $90 USD per day – some may even charge more. On top of the daily fee, you will also need to put down a deposit for the car, which would usually start at $200 USD give or take a few.

Best practice dictates that you should make reservations beforehand. Unfortunately most of these Cuban car rental companies don't have their own websites. However, you can make your reservations via other websites. Example of which are:

http://www.cuba-junky.com/cuba/carrental.html

and

http://www.havanautos.com/homecars2.aspx

If you don't like those two sites, then you can make a quick Google search using "Cuba rent a car" as your search term will yield more than a million results.

If you do rent a car, online or otherwise, just remember that it will cost you several hundred dollars. Mind your budget.

Cuban Taxi Service

Cuban taxis aren't the best taxis in the world. It's also not the cheapest mode of transport. However, they can become your most convenient option. You can ask the driver to stop any time (don't worry about the meter it won't run on you stacking up the cost of your fare). You can take a break from road trip, have snacks, take pictures, and these Cuban taxis are usually super cool. The drivers are cool too and depending on your haggling skills you can even get a discount.

In fact, if your negotiation skills are pretty good, you can even hire the driver to drive you for the entire day for a little over $120. At least you have someone who knows how to get you to places you want to go to.

For short trips, it can cost you some $10 at least. For trips that last for one or two hours, expect to pay $70 at least in fares. That will be pretty much the equivalent of a regular bus ticket. It's a private car experience versus a jam packed bus ride – take your pick.

Chapter 5: Where to Go and What to Do

Cuba is a small and beautiful country. That makes it quite a nice vacation getaway. Now, before we go through to the where of the place, let's begin with the when. When would be the best time to visit the country?

You can actually plan your trip to Cuba any time of the year since the temperature range is usually very pleasant from 70 to 80+ degrees all year round. There is a storm season that I would advise you to avoid starting from June to October – the hurricanes in this country can be a bit of a problem. Those are also the months where there are really heavy rains. Surprisingly, the hottest months in this country are from July to August.

The tourists from different parts of the world usually flock to the country from December through March (avoiding the rainy season). Expect a lot of Canadians coming over too – they're trying to escape the winter in the north (please excuse the pun).

Places to Visit in Cuba

The main places to visit in Cuba are Havana, Varadero, Viñales, and Trinidad. Here are our recommendations for each of these destinations.

A Trip to Havana

You can't go on a trip to Cuba without visiting the capital of Havana. Old Havana or what is locally referred to as Havana Viejos is a UNESCO World Heritage Site. If you're into visiting historic sites then this is probably one of those places you wouldn't want to miss. You'll enjoy the old architecture, the classic cars, and of course those wonderful Cuban cigars.

You can go on a car tour – rent a car and tour the city or hire a taxi and ask the cab driver to drive you around. A one hour tour will cost you some $30 though. Expect the taxi cab tour to be more expensive than your regular fare.

The streets here are usually busy and of course dusty – but that's pretty much how it is around here in this country. If you want a rather strong welcome, don't forget to sample the local rum – they only cost 6 CUC. You can call it your initiation rites – you can throw in a Cuban cigar while you're at it.

Havana Day Tours

One way to get the most out of your visit to Havana is to go on a day tour. Some of them you can book online while others you have to call to make your reservations.

I Love Cuba Guided Photo Tours

- Address: Varadero, Matanzas, Havana, Cuba
- Phone: 52932057
- Email: yoselvazquez@yahoo.com
- Website: ilovecuba.webs.com

Locally Sourced Havana Tours

- Address: | and Boulevard de San Rafael, Havana 10100, Cuba
- Phone: +53 5 3414873
- Website: havanatourcompany.com/havana-tours/

Havana Journeys - Day Tours

- Address: Havana, Cuba
- Phone: +49 1520 5769776
- Website: havanajourneys.com

Fertours 2 Havana

- Address: Havana, Cuba
- Phone: +53 5 2716015
- Website: fertours2havana.com

Nosotros Cubaneamos

- Address: Paseo del Prado 422 e, Havana 10400, Cuba
- Phone: +53 5 3198561
- Website: nosotroscubaneamos.com

Havana Top Attractions

The following is a list of top attractions in Havana. Topping the list is Old Havana:

1. Habana Vieja (also spelled as Havana Vieja) or Old Havana – as stated earlier, this place is a UNESCO World Heritage site. It features Baroque and other Neoclassical buildings gracing its grounds. Examples of such types of architecture include the Catedral de San Cristobal, Castillo de la Real Fuerza, Plaza Vieja, Plaza de Armas, Palacio de los Capitanes, Museo de la Ciudad, camera obscura (the tower), and the La Bodeguita del Medio.

2. The Malecón – great place to stroll and a charming view of the sunset is a classic here. This popular boulevard is 7 kilometers away from Old Havana.

3. Castillo de los Tres Reyes del Morro – also called El Morro for short, this is a fortress that used to shield the bay against pirates. This is a must see place for those who love architecture. This 17th

goliath will be a treat for history buffs and anyone who has any love for pirates and swashbuckling in general.

Other attractions in Havana include:

- Fortaleza de San Carlos de la Cabana
- Museo de Comandancia del Che
- El Capitolio (National Capitol Building)
- Museo Nacional de Bellas Artes
- Paseo del Prado
- Palacio de los Matrimonios
- Gran Teatro de La Habana
- Parque Central
- Fusterlandia
- Museo Napoleonico
- Universidad de La Habana
- Plaza de la Revolucion
- Jose Marti Memorial
- Museo de la Revolucion
- Miramar
- Acuario Nacional (Aquarium)
- Maqueta de La Havana
- Museo del Ministerio del Interior
- Playas del Este
- Santa Maria del Mar
- Guanabo

A Trip to Varadero

Varadero is your go to place in Cuba for some great fun under the sun. The place is located 140 kilometers from

Havana. It is a popular resort town, which is why a lot of tourists flock to it.

If you love ivory powder white sand beaches then this is the place to find lots of them. Note however that a lot of the beaches here are already owned by private resorts – that means you will have to pay to get on the beach. Nevertheless, there are free public beaches here too – don't worry, the public beaches are just as good as the private ones.

There are lots of fun things to do in Varadero like scuba diving, swimming, snorkeling, sailing, getting a tan, dolphin encounters, and pretty much anything you can do under the sun.

1. Varadero Beach – a lot of people have descried this as the best beach in the Caribbean. Of course that fact is definitely arguable. This beach is 20 kilometers long – which should be enough room for every beach bum visiting Cuba but alas, it can still get crowded during the high season.

2. Saturno Cave – this cave is located near the airport. If you love cave hunting then this place could be one of the first things you would like to visit after getting settled into your choice of accommodations. It features a subterranean pool, which is a great escape from the scorching heat of the sun outside.

3. Parque Josone – this is a man-made oasis that was built back in the 1940s. It's a nice romantic respite from the hustle and bustle of Varadero. You can rent a boat and paddle around in the surrounding lake (yes, the park is in the middle of a lake).

Other Attractions in Varadero include the following:

- Mansión Xanadú
- Parque Ecológico Varahicacos (Varadero Ecological Park)
- Delfinario
- Cayo Piedra Underwater Park
- Varadero Museum

A Trip to Viñales

Are you interested in sampling the best tobacco in the world? Well, you have come to the right place. Viñales is the country's capital for tobacco production. The place is a lush green valley with a small town nestled amongst the greenery. Other than the cigars, tourists visit Viñales for rock climbing, cave exploration, and nature trekking.

Here are some of the best things to do and sites to visit:

1. Climb the mountains of the Viñales – if you're scared of heights well, at the very least hike one mountain or nearby hill. The town itself is ideally flat – which is why running, walking, and

cycling is a bit popular here. However, the surrounding area around the valley has all its mountainous splendor. If you are into rock climbing and all that dangerous stuff then you will enjoy the challenge provided by the nearby limestone mountain. Ask for a guide to take you there. Don't worry about the climbing gear – there are outfitters in town that can provide you with it.

2. If going up mountains isn't your thing then maybe going under them might appeal to you. There are a lot of cave systems in the nearby mountains. Again this is not something that you should do alone. You should hire a guide to take you there and walk you through the different caves. The Cuevas del Indio (Indian Caves) are perfect for beginners. If you are interested in a full-fledged trek underground (not for the faint of heart and inexperienced though) you should try the trek through the Gran Caverna de Santo Tomás. It's a full 15 kilometer underground adventure – this is the largest cave system in Cuba. You will need 2 solid hours of underground trekking.

3. Nature trekking in and around Viñales – the entire town and surrounding valley is actually a national park. If you don't like climbing or going under the mountains – aka stay away from the dangerous things – then a stroll around the area is the perfect thing to do. It even helps you get

in touch with Mother Nature and you get to meet and greet with the locals as well. Don't forget to bring your water. Remember that the country is a hot tropical paradise – and hot is sometimes spelled with a capital H.

4. Botanico de Viñales – since you're going on a nature hike anyway, take time to visit the town's Botanical Gardens. You can even sample the fruits straight from the tropical plants and trees they're growing here. The tour around the gardens is absolutely free but the guide will at least expect a tip – please keep that in mind.

5. Don't Miss Salsa Night – with such a small town in the middle of a huge valley, it is easy to imagine that there would only be limited entertainment options come sun down. That is why the local folks here gather to Centro Cultural Polo Montanez on Saturday night! It's salsa night baby! The drinks are flooding and the night is hot with everyone in the groove. But if you've got two left feet like me you can just watch the locals go at it and enjoy your drink and talk with the people or you can ask them to teach you a dance move or two.

A Trip to Trinidad

Trinidad is an old colonial town that is quite picturesque. You'll love the cobblestone streets and the houses that have been painted in pastel colors. A little history tip – back in the 18th century, this town was the center of sugar trade when Cuba was under the colonial rule of Spain. Those were the days when sugar barons became filthy rich and African slave labor was the main thing of the day.

The good news is that those old practices are practically gone now. However, the buildings and sugar mills here have been restored to their original splendor. Here are some of the best things to see and do while you're in Trinidad:

1. Watch the sunset in Plaza Mayor. Order a mojito while you're at it.
2. Take a trip to Topes De Collantes National Park and swim under the waterfalls.
3. Enjoy the white sand beaches of Playa Ancon – if you're not into frolicking in the water then at least rent a bike and enjoy the scenery change from one scene to another as you go.
4. Enjoy the overlooking views at Iglesia de San Francisco. No, you're not just going to sit in church and sweat like a sinner – you're going to sweat alright while climbing up the old bell tower. That's where you're getting the nice scenic views of the surroundings.
5. Are you into the arts? Two places you shouldn't miss are Museo Romantico and Museo de Arquitectura.

Note that these are only some of the many attractions when you roam around Cuba. There are also attractions that are off the beaten path. You basically have to ask around to find them. Note however that you should avoid the scams that a few of the locals can pull on you. We'll go over that in a minute.

Chapter 6: Where to Eat in Cuba

Before we go over the where to eat, you should at least know what to eat. That means when in Cuba you should eat like the Cubans. There are a few quintessential dishes that you should really try in Cuba. They include stewed black beans, tomato simmered beef, fried plantains, grilled lobster, milk flan, chicken cooked in rice, and a home grown Cuban sandwich.

When you're in a restaurant, try to ask for the following dishes:

- Cubano sandwich
- Arroz Amarillo con Pollo
- Milk flan
- Tostones
- Mariquitas or Malanga Chips
- Grilled Lobster
- Moros y Cristianos
- Ropa Vieja

Best Restaurants in Havana

Here are our top picks for the best restaurants in Havana:

San Juan Bar & Grill

- Latin and Caribbean bar
- San Juan de Dios #9 | E/ Habana y Aguiar, Habana Vieja, Havana, Cuba
- +53 7 8647422
- Moderately priced

Habana 61

- Cuban seafood grill
- Calle Habana No. 61 | entre las calles Cuarteles y Peña Pobre, Havana
- +53 7 8016433
- Moderately priced

La Guarida

- Concordia. No. 418 | Gervasio y Escobar, Havana 10700, Cuba
- +53 7 8669047
- Serves Latin, Caribbean, and international
- Fine dining

Restaurante Cafe del Oriente

- Oficios # 112 | entre Amargura y Lamparilla, La Habana Vieja, Havana 10100, Cuba
- +53 7 8012686
- Serves Latin, Caribbean, and international
- Fine dining

Restaurant Van Van

- 58 San Juan de Dios | e/ Habana y Compostela, Havana, Cuba
- +53 7 8602490
- Serves Caribbean, Latin, Cuban
- Cheap eats

El Dandy

- Street Brasil # 401 corner Sreet Villegas | Plaza de Cristo in Old Havana, Havana
- +53 7 8676463
- Latin, Bar, Café
- Cheap eats

Restaurant Top Picks in Varadero

The following are our top picks among the many restaurants in Varadero.

Salsa Suarez Restaurant y Bar

- Pizza, International, Fusion
- Calle 31 No. 103 e/ 1ra y 3ra Ave., Varadero 42200, Cuba
- +53 45 614194
- Moderately priced

Varadero 60

- Serves Caribbean, Seafood, Cuban
- St. and 3th Ave. 60 | Calle 60 Esquina a 3ra Avenida, Varadero 42200, Cuba
- +53 45 613986
- Moderately priced

Xanadu

- Serves Caribbean, Seafood, Cuban
- Varadero Golf Course | DuPont Mansion, Varadero 42200, Cuba
- +53 45 668482
- Splurge

Restaurant La Arcada

- Serves European cuisine
- Melia Las Americas, Varadero 42200, Cuba
- +53 45 667600 ext. 629
- Splurge

Calle 62

- Serves Caribbean, Latin, Bar
- Calle 62, Varadero 42200, Cuba
- Cheap eats

Kiki's

- Serves Italian, Pizza, Vegetarian Friendly
- Avenida kawama calle 5, Varadero 42200, Cuba
- +53 45 614115
- Cheap eats

Chapter 7: Internet in Cuba

Is there internet in Cuba? Don't be surprised to find that the answer to that question is a resounding yes. There is internet in Cuba but it's not the best in the world. The country was one of the least connected nations in the world – well, considering how things are today, it is safe to say that it is still one of the least connection nations in the world.

Note that the Cuban government does censor some websites – like anti-government sites and, for whatever reason, Snapchat. The country has a state run telecom called ETECSA. To get connected you need to buy prepaid WiFi cards from ETECSA. You can buy these cards in kiosks and you will be paying somewhere from $2 to $3 per hour of internet.

The internet service of course is provisioned through hotels, public parks and others businesses around the country. You scratch off at the back of the card to reveal a user name and password so you can enter an ETECSA WiFi network.

On average, a card would cost you $6 per piece (now they're at $1.50 per card due to recent competition, please see below). You can even buy them at any hotel that has internet or maybe in a café that also has internet. Is the internet in Cuba top notch? Of course not. But you can use it to upload photos on Instagram and Facebook. You can use to chat. It's not going to be stellar if you try to use the internet for video chat or to stream videos or something of that sort.

3G Signal via Digicel

Now, here's an update – 3G internet has now come to Cuba, which is an upgrade for most people in the country. The service is provisioned through Digicel Cuba through their Digicel Cuba Roaming service.

To get 3G service, you need to order their SIM cards and you can use them on your phones. There is a registration process that you need to follow when you get to Cuba – yes, the registration process is cued when you dial *120# on your phone with the Digicel SIM inserted. Note that this process will only work when you're in Cuba.

The good news is that Amazon sells Digicel Roaming SIM cards for $25. It comes pre-loaded with 100 mb of data. You can check out the details of the SIM card from Amazon here:

https://www.amazon.com/Digicel-Cuba-Roaming-Pre-Loaded-Data/dp/B06W51KYL7

If you want to check out the details of how the 3G roaming service works, go here:

https://www.digicelcubaroaming.com/

Now, what if you need some help connecting to the internet? The good news is that there is now a help center in Cuba – told you times are changing in that country. You can contact their help center by calling 407-499-2822 (that's their customer care number). You can also send an email to CubaRoamingHelp@digicelgroup.com however, we just don't know how soon are their response times – it varies.

Chapter 8: Scams to Avoid – Keeping Safe in Cuba

Will people try to scam you in Cuba? Well, wherever people are desperate and in terrible need you should expect some people to do anything to provide for their needs. And that includes scamming tourists. Here are a few scams that people there pull on tourists that you should be aware of.

1. National day of [insert whatever holiday they may think of]

Some local Cuban comes over to you very jolly and asks you when you arrived in town. You politely reply "today" or maybe "yesterday" or some other day. And then he tells you that you're in luck coz today is [whatever holiday they may think of or maybe it's a real holiday]. Any rate, they will then tell you that they are offering something new – a product or service etc. – and it's at a slashed down price. What a find, it's a big discount – not! It's a scam. They may even be black market goods. The price is actually jacked.

How to respond: Do not humor him. Give the usual pleasantries and tell him that you don't need it or want it. But then you can also ask him something that you really need – maybe an available casa or a place to eat. The guy will then nose you along to the right place. At least you're helping him earn his keep in a legit way.

2. Leche Con

A jinitero may approach you pleading his case and he or she will just ask you to buy his baby some milk. You may think that hey it's just $20. It's a scam – the milk is prepackaged and the store where he /she will take you is conniving in the scam. You can actually buy the milk for $1 or less.

3. We have no change for that sir ("Lo siento, no cambio")

This is a trick they pull to get you to buy more so they can have enough change for your money. They tell you they have no change but you can buy this or that so whatever change they have in the machine will be enough.

How to respond: Just tell the shop owner that you'll just get your stuff elsewhere – surprisingly the change magically appears!

4. Overpriced coffee or whatever

You should always check the actual prices of the goods sold. Do some comparison shopping first before you sit down and pay for something. For instance, some may charge you $6 for a cup of coffee – that's absurd because it only costs $1 or less.

5. Cheap Stuff!

The prices may even go the other way. For instance, if you buy cigars, some street vendor may offer you a box for 3 times the usual price in the official store or at the plantation. Don't fall for it and don't fall for the official looking packaging. The thing may be stuffed with banana leaves. On top of that, customs will confiscate fakes when you leave the country. If the price is too good to be true, then it is too good to be true.

6. Haggle for casa room rates

Remember that casa particulares room rates are from $20 to $30 a night (some even go down as low as $10). Go for $10! Why? Because they're still the same room whether you pay $10 or $30. Pick up some haggling skills.

Conclusion

I hope that this travel guide was able to help you appreciate the wonders of this time encapsulated country. May you also capture the romance, the ideal of freedom, and the plight of the people for a better tomorrow. Most of all, may you also enjoy a wonderful Cuban vacation and frolic in the sun.

HAVANA

TRAVEL GUIDE
CUBA LIBRE!

Let the Cultural History of
Havana Guide You Through the
Authentic Soul of the City

CARLOS FERNANDO ALVAREZ

BOOK 3

HAVANA TRAVEL GUIDE

Cuba Libre!

Let the Cultural History of Havana Guide You Through the Authentic Soul of the City

Carlos Fernando Alvarez

Table of Contents

Introduction

You have to admit that Havana is no ordinary place on earth. It is unique in its own right even when compared to the other Caribbean islands. A lot of things have shaped the place, well, not only this city but also the entire country of Cuba as well. A lot of political movements, artistic influxes, migration, and a unique blend of colonization have chipped in to shape Havana to what it is today.

For a lot of people the city becomes a historic travel back in time. Add to that the natural landscapes and the vibrant culture makes the city a good place to find some quiet time and forget the world.

So, why visit Havana?

It is a good introduction to Cuba. You have the romantic glamor of Spanish colonial influence – the linguistic and the cultural influence is very pronounced here. It's not just Spanish influence here though. There is a good deal of American and socialist dogma which make the place a potpourri of attitudes and complex worldviews, which makes the people peculiar and interesting.

However, again, it's not just the people though. Art lovers and those who dig baroque and classical architecture will love what they will see here. Are you a nature lover? The city caters to your tastes too. The surrounding landscape and places of interest off the beaten path keep you in touch with Mother Nature. Caves, the nearby mountains, and of course the beaches with their powdery white sands – those are the things that attract people who want to escape the mundane concrete jungles of the world.

It's a drop off point.

A lot of tourists have been enjoying the wonders of Cuba for decades (apologies to our American friends – yes, you may have missed out on all the fun due to your country's travel ban). Well, Havana is where you land in Cuba and you can begin your adventure here – so our American brothers and sisters can finally catch up to the rest of the world by starting here. From Havana you can travel to the many tourist attractions in Cuba.

Enjoy the city's charms and old world appeal!

Chapter 1 – Places to See and Things to Do

Why visit Havana? For one thing, history and Havana are two things that go together. Other than the full Spanish conjecture you will get, the place is rather picturesque and fun. Havana is a city that was made to be strolled. The fiestas are a pretty good reason to visit but the city actually offers you a lot more.

Havana Day Tours

Want to get a bird's eye view of the entire city? Well, it's a bit of a short cut but day tours give you just that. You have a 50s style vintage car with a driver to take you to the best places to see in Havana. You can actually do this on your first day here in the city. Your driver can also tell you where to go to next. You can get some tourist tips too like great bars to hang out, where to get souvenirs, and the best places to eat.

The good news is that there are day tour companies in Havana that can be booked online. Some of these companies run their own websites while others are listed in third party sites. Here are our recommendations:

Locally Sourced Havana Tours

- Address: Boulevard de San Rafael, Havana 10100, Cuba

- Phone: +53 5 3414873
- Website: havanatourcompany.com/havana-tours/

Nosotros Cubaneamos

- Address: Paseo del Prado 422 e, Havana 10400, Cuba
- Phone: +53 5 3198561
- Website: nosotroscubaneamos.com

I Love Cuba Guided Photo Tours

- Address: Varadero, Matanzas, Havana, Cuba
- Phone: 52932057
- Email: yoselvazquez@yahoo.com
- Website: ilovecuba.webs.com

Fertours 2 Havana

- Address: Havana, Cuba
- Phone: +53 5 2716015
- Website: fertours2havana.com

Havana Journeys - Day Tours

- Address: Havana, Cuba
- Phone: +49 1520 5769776
- Website: havanajourneys.com

Top Attractions

Here are our best picks of the many attractions in Havana. Additional details about these attractions will be covered in later sections.

1. The Malecón

The Malecón is a wide boulevard along the seaside area of Havana. It is a long stretch of road where you'll find bars, restaurants, sites, and scenes that are picture perfect. We cover the many sites and places to be on the Malecón in a separate chapter.

2. Castillo de los Tres Reyes del Morro

This used to be defensive structure against pirates back in the 17th century. The lighthouse is still a great monument to see and visit. The fort itself is open to visitors where you can take really great panoramic pictures.

3. Fortaleza de San Carlos de la Cabana

A short distance from El Morro, this is the biggest Spanish port ever built. It stands atop what is known as the La Cabana Hill. This fort is the dominant structure that stands over the Havana Bay.

This fort is quite historic. For instance, during the Batista regime it served as a military prison. Nowadays a lot of the country's history is kept intact within its walls via the museums in the structure. One of the

museums in this fort is Museo de Comandancia del Che
– here is where you can find the Che Guevara's office
and it has been left as it was since his days here.

The nights in this fort come alive with the Ceremonia
del Cañonazo. Tourists usually come here to see the
night time plays with actors clad in their very own 19th
century costumes. The performances start at 9 in the
evening so you better get your dinners done in a hurry
before then.

4. El Capitolio (National Capitol Building)

Those who have been to Washington DC will recognize
the style of this building. Yes, the two buildings are very
much alike. Of course El Capitolio was built much later
in 1959. The architectural style is a blend of Art
Nouveau and neoclassical architecture. Of course, the
Cubans will argue that Capitol Building in DC is not the
inspiration for El Capitolio but the Pantheon in Paris.
It remains as one of the most striking landmark in the
entire city of Havana. You wander around and you can
still see the dome of this building pretty much
anywhere you go.

5. Museo Nacional de Bellas Artes

This museum is spread across two different buildings.
The first building is called the Palacio del Centro
Asturiano which was designed by Manuel Bustos in
the 1920s. it houses European art dating from
Egyptian to the Roman ages.

The other building is called the Palacio de Bellas Artes
and this one houses the museum's Cuban art

collection. The artworks housed here date from the 17th century to the present. The collections include a variety of artworks from paintings to sculptures. If you are an art lover and would love to see the best in Cuban art then this is the place to be.

6. Paseo del Prado

This street is considered by many to be the most beautiful street in all of Havana. It is one of those tree lined city streets that deserves a good stroll. It proffers many opportunities to make great pictures – you know the kind that would make your friends wish they were there with you.

You can actually consider this as the grand boulevard in Havana that was drawn out of a bygone era. Here you will find cinemas, mansions, bronze lions, old hotels, marble benches, and iron lamp posts that easily transports you back in time to their former splendour.

7. Gran Teatro de La Habana

It can come as a surprise to find a grand theatre house in Havana. The baroque façade of this building which was designed by Paul Belau will come be a big treat for lovers of ancient architecture. The sculptures at the building's entrance were crafted by Giuseppe Moretti.

8. Fusterlandia

This is actually located at Havana's outskirts. You will have to make the effort to get here. You can call it a piece of neighborhood art. What is amazing about it is that the art works here are three dimensional and they present a rhapsody of colors. The mosaics were created by José Fuster a local sculptor and painter who is himself quite brilliant.

Fuster also exhibits his skills through his creations in the many public areas in town. All in all, the place along with its unique displays is a quirky trip in the arts.

9. Museo Napoleonico

Well, it's not like Napoleon decided to dump his stuff in Cuba. This museum actually houses the private collection of Julio Lobo who was a collector of all things Napoleon. Lobo's collection was purchased by the Cuban government in 1959. The collection is pretty impressive. It even includes a lock of the man's hair and they also have one of his teeth.

Havana's Beaches

Of course, you can't have some fun in the sun without going to the beach. The beaches of Havana become pretty popular during the summer months. The good news is that Cuba is that close to the equator that it would seem that it is always beach season all year round. Of course you need to take shelter during the rainy months but it would still be warm enough to hit the sand (just remember to take shelter when it rains).

Without further ado, here is our selection of the best beaches in Havana.

1. Santa María Del Mar

This is actually the biggest and not to mention the best known beach near Havana. This strip of beach runs a full 9 kilometers. If you take a taxi, getting there will take about 20 minutes from Havana's city center, which means it isn't really that far. Note that it will be a tough job trying to find an empty spot on this beach from From June until August – it can be really crowded. The best months to visit this beach when it is really pretty are in the months of May and October.

2. Playa Boca Ciega

If you want to escape the crowds then this is the beach for you. It is less crowded and it is really popular with the locals. It is only a s short distance along the coast from Santa Maria Del Mar.

3. Playa Guanabo

This is also another beach that is popular among the locals. It is located on a village just on the outskirts of Havana. The village and the beach themselves are quite rustic and untouched by the insanities of the modern world. You may even call it as a little slice of paradise especially if you want to get some time out from the chaos of modern living.

4. Playa Bacuranao

This is the closest beach to Havana's city proper. If you need a quick escape to the sun and sand then consider this beach. However, do take note that this beach isn't as popular as the other Havana beaches simply because the sand is not as smooth – well, they're a bit rocky but the beach itself has its own charms.

5. Playa El Salado

The name of this beach translates to "salty beach." Again not as popular as the other beaches but the water here has a higher salt content, that may be good for your skin. Again, if you want to escape the beach crowd, this is another great option.

Havana Diving

If scuba diving is your thing, then remember that there are three international dive centers here in Havana. They include the Tarara Marina, which you will find in the eastern beaches, Copacabana in Miramar, and La Aguja located in the Hemingway Marina.

The dive sites here run parallel to Havana's coasts and they are at 5 to 35 meter depths. They include small caves, ship wrecks, and other sites. It will take half a day to dive and the best place to schedule a trip is during the daytime in the morning. Dive prices range from $33.74 to $516 depending on the dive site and the gear you're going to use.

Chapter 2 – Where to Stay

There are two types of accommodations that you will find in Havana. The first and cheaper option is in casas particulares. The second one is in hotels. Well, the hotel option can also be divided into two classes – hotels that are wholly owned by the government and the other class of hotels includes the ones that are owned by private companies (e.g. international chains).

What are Casas Particulares?

The term casas particulares literally translates to "private home" from Spanish. Back in 1977 the Cuban government began to allow families in their country to rent out their rooms and other personal spaces to tourists and foreigners visiting their country. They had to register their homes as privately owned businesses.

That was an economic move on the part of the government since they will be able to raise funds in the form of taxes. Those who owned casas particulares are required to fill out tax forms, report their incomes, and of course pay their taxes accordingly.

On the part of the owners of these private homes this was an opportunity towards economic freedom. This was all thanks to the Castro Administration integrating certain precepts of capitalism into the framework of socialist Cuba. That is actually one of the few economic reforms that the administration has allowed. Cubans nowadays can also open restaurants, run their local hotels (and hotel chains if they had the capital for it), and even travel overseas.

Now, that's enough of politics. So, casas particulares are home stays – they're what you can call your private B&B in Cuba. You actually get more privacy from a casa particular compared to your average home stay. For instance, the family that owns the place will usually just leave you alone but they will also be happy to provide what you request.

They don't expect you to interact with them 24/7 since they know you are there to see and experience life in Havana. However, if you need someone to chat with, find directions, or need help with something, the family will be there for you. But generally they leave you alone and provide you with lots of privacy.

So, how do you know if a home is a registered casa particular? Well, these homes don't actually have big signs on their yards (a lot of them don't even have yards). But here's a hint – you will see an upside down anchor marking the house – usually at the entrance. It's not always that big. Sometimes you can find this symbol at the front door. That's how the government marks registered homes as a casa particular.

How much does staying in a casa particular cost?

It varies from one place to another. Some charge more than others. A good price range will be anywhere from $10 to $30 a night. However, don't be surprised to find a casa that charges up to $40.

TIP: choose a casa according to room quality – some owners stick to the 10 to 20 dollar range (or CUC range) and still give you about the same room quality as that of a $40 room. Food costs in casas are only a fraction of the price they charge in restaurants (state owned or otherwise). Meals will cost you from $5 to $10 while mojitos and other drinks will cost you $2 to $3 (or 2 to 3 CUC). Note however that a lot of casas don't serve breakfast so you better start looking for a good breakfast place in town.

How do you book a casa particular?

Finding one and booking one shouldn't be a problem nowadays in Havana. You can call them in advance or send an email to the owner to book your stay. You can also arrange for them to pick you up from the airport – you should definitely arrange for a pickup because finding the casa you booked will be like finding a needle in a haystack if it's your first time in Havana.

Unfortunately these casa particular owners don't really operate their own websites. It's either they don't have the info tech capabilities or they can't afford it. Now, the good news is that sites like Airbnb and Booking.com and other third party sites now list Cuba and that definitely includes casa particulares. You can even find reviews on some of these sites and you can also leave a review yourself in case you have stayed in a casa that is listed on site.

Here are our recommended casas particulares in Havana:

Casa Ambos Mundos

This casa is right next to Flordita Bar, which has a public WiFi. It is also close to other tourist hotspots in Old Havana.

- Address: Villegas #211, e/ Obispo y Obrapia, Habana Vieja, Cuba
- Rooms: 3
- Phone: +53 53687501
- Amenities: private bathroom, extra bed upon request, Queen size bed, breakfast and dinner, mini bar, air conditioning, laundry service.

Casa Bolsa de la Habana

This place is only a walking distance to Havana's Old Square. It is a great option for families. They also have a large living room area.

- Address: Obrapia #257 e/ Aguiar and Cuba, Habana Vieja (Old Havana)
- Phone: +5358139298
- Rooms: 2
- Modalities: Colonial, , Urban Quiet, Romantic
- Amenities: Italian speaking, English speaking, Laundry service, Private entrance, Ceiling fan, Balcony, Breakfast service, Minibar, Kingsize bed, Dinner service, Private bathroom, Queensize bed, Bathroom with shower.

La Casa de Juan y Blanca

This casa is centrally located and is near many places of interest in Old Havana like Plaza Vieja, Plaza de Armas, and Plaza de la Catedral. The place is very private and quiet – a great escape from the noise after a busy day.

- Address: Villegas #10 e/ Tejadillo and Empedrado, Habana Vieja, Cuba
- Rooms: 2
- Phone: +53 7 8613117
- Amenities: Private entrance, English speaking, Balcony, Laundry service, Breakfast service, Air condition, Queen size bed, TV, Private bathroom.

Hostal Dona Cristina

This casa is also within Old Havana. If you like to see more of the historic places and museums this casa may be a good option since it is ideally located.

- Address: Luz 109 apto 9, e/ San Ignacio Street & Inquisidor Street, Habana Vieja, Cuba
- Rooms: 1
- Phone: +53 7 8676373
- Languages: English and Spanish
- Amenities: Airconditioning, Balcony, TV, Dinner service, Private bathroom, Queensize bed, Extra bed available, Bathroom with shower

Casa Las Mercedes B&B

This casa takes on a more modern look and it does feel like a regular B&B. It is located only two blocks away from Plaza Vieja. It is located at the heart of Havana.

- Address: Calle Sol #212 apt 11, e/ Cuba y Aguiar, Habana Vieja, Cuba
- Languages: Spanish, English
- Phone: +53 58184829
- Rooms: 2
- Amenities: Gay friendly, , Extra bed, Parking service, Balcony, Laundry service, Ceiling fan, Air conditioning, Safety box, Minibar, TV, Breakfast service, Bathroom with shower, Queen size bed

Casa Aleida

This casa has a rather homey appeal to it. It is located along a side street of Calle Obispo, which kind of make it hard to find. The rooms have a patio and there is a terrace on the first floor. The owner, Aleida, is a helpful yet funny lady and she's very welcoming.

- Address: Compostela #310-B, Bajos, e/ Obispo y Obrapia , Habana Vieja, Cuba
- Phone: +53 7 684679
- Amenities: Private bathroom, Air conditioning, Sunbeds, Terrace, Breakfast and dinner service, Patio, Laundry service

Casa Ana y Surama

This is a colonial style casa which easily transports you back to Cuba's Spanish era. The building itself was built in 1925, which lends to its old world charm.

- Address: Address: San Ignacio #454, e/ Sol y Santa Clara, Habana Vieja, Cuba
- Rooms: 3
- Phone: +53 78622717
- Amenities: Air conditioning, English speaking, TV, Breakfast service, Bathroom with tub, Queen size bed, Bathroom with shower

Casa de Argelio Brito

If you're looking for a more modern apartment, then this casa might be a good option. It is located in Old Havana and Morro Castle. There are also dozens of restaurants and bars nearby.

- Address: Calle Compostela #530 - 2º Piso - Apto. 7 /e Brasil (Teniente Rey) y Murall, Habana Vieja, Cuba
- Amenities: Bathroom with shower, Air conditioning, Dinner service, Breakfast service, Private bathroom, Laundry service, TV, Queen size bed
- Phone: +53 7 8671150

Casa Atardecer

This is another great option if you plan to visit the sites and other points of interest in Old Havana. It's a homey and cozy house that offers a quiet and private getaway from the street.

- Address: Villegas #211 altos, e/ Obispo y Obrapia, Habana Vieja, Cuba
- Languages: Spanish, English, Italian
- Phone: +53 78672162
- Amenities: Air conditioning, Balcony, Dinner service, Breakfast service, Private bathroom, TV, Bathroom with shower

Bohemia Boutique Apartment

This is another apartment that has really colonial looks. Note that the place is fully furnished with modern amenities. This is one of those casas that you can rent on a per month basis.

- Address: San Ignacio #364, entre Muralla y Teniente Rey, Plaza Vieja, Habana Vieja / Old Havana, Cuba
- Capacity: 2 people
- Phone: +53 54031568
- Amenities: Italian speaking, French speaking, English speaking, Laundry service, Private entrance, Air conditioning, Balcony, Minibar, Ceiling fan, King size bed, Safety box, Bathroom with shower, Private bathroom, Extra bed available

Havana's Hotel Options

There are five principal hotel chains in all of Cuba and they run most of the hotels in every town and city.

Some of these chains also operate beach resorts too. The budget hotels are run by the Islazul Chain – note that their hotels are usually poorly maintained. In spite of such poor care and service they charge at least twice than a regular casa particular.

The Cubanacan Chain runs most of the mid-priced hotels in the country. Note that some of these hotels can be a bit pricey even though they are classified as mid-priced. However, they make up to it by providing top not amenities and services. Their Encanto brand establishments are particularly noteworthy.

The Gaviota and Gran Caribe chains serve the upper market – so expect the prices to be stellar (which can leave a big dent in your budget). The good news is that their hotels are housed in prestigious buildings (though a lot of them are past their prime). On top of that, their hotels are situated in really prime locations.

The Habaguanex Chain is a state run hotel chain. Their hotels are reliably attractive and their lodgings are usually well-maintained. Even the colonial buildings that they converted into hotels have been beautifully restored. Their hotels are exclusive to Havana. Expect prices to be steep though but you are getting your money's worth from hotels from this chain.

TIP: when you call in to inquire about booking a room, it would be a great idea to ask which hotel chain runs the place. At least you will have a pretty good idea how things really are.

The following are our recommended hotels in Havana:

Melia Habana

- Ave 3era, e/ 76 y 80 | Miramar Playa, Havana 11300, Cuba
- (080) 011 5248
- Free parking
- Pool

This is one of the well-kept hotels in the area. The rooms are spacious and are kept clean. The hotel also runs a courtesy bus service that can drive you to different destinations. Airport pickups are provided too. Their breakfast options are also quite commendable.

Hotel Iberostar Parque Central

- *Address*: Neptuno e/ Prado y Zulueta, Habana Vieja, Ciudad de la Habana, Old Havana, Havana, Cuba
- *Distance to city center*: 0 km
- *Number of Rooms*: 427
- *Distance to Airport*: 30 km

This hotel is ideally located in Havana within Central Park. It combines old colonial styles with 21st century chic interiors and architecture. Note that this is actually a 5 star hotel. It is right in the heart of the densely populated area of the city and the surrounding area is culturally vibrant. That means you can find a lot of the points of interest and attractions nearby.

Hotel Telegrafo

- Calle Prado 408, Havana 10100, Cuba

This is actually one of the highly rated hotels in Havana. It is on a great location at the center of Havana near many of the tourist attractions and it is also near the city's capital. Breakfast buffets are pretty good fare.

Hotel Palacio del Marques de San Felipe y Santiago de Bejucal

- Oficios 152 esq a Amargura, Plaza San Francisco de Asis, Havana, Cuba
- Breakfasts included
- Non-smoking rooms
- Air conditioning

This hotel is near the historic center in Havana and it is right on the plaza. The breakfasts are commendable and the rooms are well furnished. Dinners are also good but you can always go to other nearby restaurants and bars.

Melia Cohiba

- Ave Paseo entre 1 y 3, Havana, Cuba
- (080) 011 5248
- Airport transfers
- Breakfast buffet
- Pool
- Non-smoking rooms

This hotel is great for weekend trips for the family. It's also a great option for company getaways. The poolside restaurant is commendable and they serve local and international fare. The rooms are spacious and clean too. You can stop by for WiFi internet and shop at their boutiques.

Saratoga Hotel

- Paseo del Prado 603 esquina Dragones, La Habana Vieja, Havana 10200, Cuba

Saratoga Hotel is one of the top 10 hotels in Havana. That also means it is one of the most expensive hotels out there. They have free WiFi, breakfast buffets, non-smoking rooms, rooftop pool, and air conditioning.

Chapter 3 – Havana Restaurants and Paladares

A visit to the city of Havana will be akin to visiting a life size time capsule. They've got 50s style cars (sometimes older), baroque styled buildings (but you will see some 70s ones too), and of course the government run (and usually ultra-expensive) restaurants.

Enter the Paladares

You can say that there are only two types of restaurants in Havana. The first one is the type that drops a huge chuck load of meat, beans, rice, and what not on your plate. The other one is the type that well doesn't. Some of these eateries are definitely more expensive than others. Here's a tip – if it's a state run eatery expect the prices to be a bit jacked up most of the time.

And then times have changed and the paladares has been gaining success in the Cuban foodie scene. What are paladares? Glad you asked.

You see, back in the 1990s, the government allowed albeit reluctantly family run food establishments to cater to tourists. This was during the post-Soviet economic crisis. It was not actually just the paladares that were allowed to operate. Other private businesses in Cuba were allowed to take root.

However, since the government did it grudgingly, they imposed really strict rules and a lot of these businesses failed. One of these businesses that came out of that single streak of opportunity was the paladares – family run restaurants as it were.

These families often just converted their homes into restaurants – which add a rather homey appeal. These enterprising souls used their life savings and also some funds borrowed from friends and family. One or a few members of the family usually have received professional training (not necessarily institutional) in the culinary arts. Some have worked under the guiding eye of some of Cuba's best chefs.

What they learned there they applied to their dishes. They even used their ingenuity to create fusions, spin offs, and original gourmet recipes from different cuisines. Unfortunately, not all of these enterprises succeeded. Some officious inspectors have pushed a good number of paladares out of business. Those that survived are rather doing well today.

That was during that decade. Moving fast forward in time to 2012, the government and its officials have had a change of heart as it were. They reopened everything again for new enterprises and this time they were more welcoming. Well, they finally realized that these small and medium enterprises have a huge contribution to the economy.

And so it was that the humble paladares have become a wonderful addition to the restaurant environment in Havana. Nowadays, if you want to sample some of the best of Cuban, Latin, Italian, and fusion dishes in Cuba, you should walk into a paladar that specializes in a particular type of cuisine.

In this chapter we'll look at some of the best of these restaurants. We have included paladares, state operated restos, and other eateries. The idea of course is to give you a good idea of the current foodie landscape in Havana.

Nao Bar Paladar

- Address: Obispo No 1 e/San Pedro y Baratillo | Old Havana, Havana, Cuba
- Phone: +53 7 8673463

If you're looking for a rustic place to enjoy some great seafood then Nao Bar may be a pretty good option. It's just a short stroll from the Old Town. The building which houses this home grown bar is, needless to say, really old – 200 years old to be exact (well, give or take a few).

The ambiance here is like eating in one of those Spanish galleons. It's a fairly small place however don't expect to get some private dining simply because the place is a bit popular. Yes, lots of tourists who love seafood eventually find their way here. On top of that, the decibels go up when the live band begins to play. Imagine that, they found a way to fit a live band! That is both wonderful and sometimes, well, you know, noisy (big grin).

So, what should you order at Nao Bar? Well, they have a pretty good selection here. However, since you're by the sea and all, why not just settle for the red snapper. Yes, you're right if you thought that's a huge chunk of lobster.

La Chucheria

- Address: Street 28 | Miramar, Havana, Cuba

- Phone: +53 7 2125013
- www.facebook.com/LaChucheriaMiramar

Don't expect to get some gourmet fine dining here in this restaurant. But you should never discount its undeniably rough charms. Fried treats are in the house and they don't make it better in Havana than they do here. The meals are inexpensive and they get served fast. It's a great place to enjoy a quick snack like ginormous sandwiches or a full dinner like pizzas and other fried delicacies.

El Cocinero

- Address: Calle 26, Vedado | Between Calle 11 and 13, Havana, Cuba
- Phone: +53 7 8322355
- Website: elcocinerocuba.com

This is one of the cool and trendy bars in Havana. It's one of the paladares that you will want to come back to time and again. What makes it even cooler is the fact that it sits atop a gallery slash gigantic night club that they call La Fabrica. It's the kind of place you want to hang out in after partying downstairs.

El Chanchullero de Tapas

- Address: Teniente Rey, 457A bajos | Plaza El Cristo Habana Vieja, Havana, Cuba
- Phone: +53 7 8014915
- Website: www.el-chanchullero.com

Cuba's Spanish heritage is truly well-pronounced – well more like tasted – here in this paladares. Again, this is one of those family owned restaurants that can be quite surprising to many tourists. Now, there are lots of paladares in Havana that serve Spanish dishes. Their signature dish of this restaurant of course is their tapas.

Doña Eutemia

- Address: Callejon del Chorro # 60-C | Plaza de la Catedral, Habana Vieja, Havana, Cuba
- Phone: +53 7 8013332

If you're looking for genuine Cuban fare then you'll find Doña Eutemia as a pretty good option. It's just off Plaza de la Catedral. Here you'll find what may be the finest frozen mojitos on this side of Cuba. The meals served here are basically the standard Cuban cuisine selections which follows beef, chicken, and pork themes.

If not for the line of people waiting to get inside, it may be a bit difficult to locate Doña Eutemia. It's hidden somewhat since you have to go into a side street to get to it. Your main landmark is the cathedral – find the side street and you're almost there or just ask around.

304 O'REILLY

- Address: #304 | Habana & Aguiar, Havana, Cuba
- Phone: +53 5 2644725

It's a tiny family restaurant but not without its charms. The place is often described as petite but atmospheric. Their fish and prawn plates are highly commended. The mango mojito is one of their better options. Pair your favorite drink with a nice lobster and your night will be more than memorable.

El Café

- Address: Amargura #358 | e/ Aguacate y Villegas, La Habana Vieja, Havana, Cuba
- Phone: +53 7 8613817

El Café can easily become your go to place for a hearty breakfast. They serve European, Cafe, and Cuban. They also offer vegan options among what is considered as one of the best sandwiches in Havana. The ambiance itself is simple yet inviting. It's something that can appeal to you if you want a rather uncomplicated day. You may find it difficult to locate this little café since it is snuggled inside the building and on top of that there is no sign outside. Again, let the crowds lead you or simply just ask the locals.

Habana 61

- Address: Calle Habana No. 61 | entre las calles Cuarteles y Peña Pobre, Havana 10100, Cuba
- Phone: +53 7 8016433

This paladares serves seafood, Cuban, and also vegetarian friendly dishes. Again, this is one of those places that reels in a queue of people forming the outside. Isn't that always a sign that there's good food in the place? The staff is very professional and the restaurant itself has a pretty good vibe. The décor is stylish and takes on a more modern theme.

Since the place does get pretty crowded you better call in to make your reservations. Great starters include ceviche and octopus carpaccio. Try the seabags too, they come very recommended. Note that this restaurant tends to get very crowded during dinner time so you better come early if you haven't made reservations.

El Dandy

- Address: Street Brasil # 401 corner Sreet Villegas | Plaza de Cristo in Old Havana, Havana, Cuba
- Phone: +53 7 8676463

This is one of the highly recommended and really popular Latin, bar, and cafés in Havana. Their cocktails are as a must – and not overrated. If you want to sample some of the best old fashioned Cuban rum, here's a good place to get them at a good price too. A pina colada is a refreshing option if you're not planning on drinking heavy.

Other than the cocktails, the tapas have also become an easy favorite. The tacos are also a favorite for light meals. The prices are reasonable and the portions are big enough to appease your appetite.

Restaurante Cafe del Oriente

- Address: Oficios # 112 | entre Amargura y Lamparilla, La Habana Vieja, Havana 10100, Cuba
- Phone: +53 7 8012686

This restaurant serves Cuban, Latin, and Caribbean. It is also one of those eateries that come out as highly rated. Dine a la carte on their patio and you get one of the perfect meals you'll ever get on this side of the planet. The décor is elegant and of course quite chic too. This is one of the few places in Havana that has a rather extensive wine collection. So, if you've had enough mojitos and want something else with your food then this might be your next favorite spot in Cuba.

San Juan Bar & Grill

- Address: San Juan de Dios #9 | E/ Habana y Aguiar, Habana Vieja, Havana, Cuba
- Phone: +53 7 8647422

This place can top anyone's Caribbean, Latin, and bar list in Havana. The place is rather quiet and is one of the most elegant places to dine in Old Havana. If you prefer the best of fine dining minus the crowd then San Juan Bar and Grill may be a great option for rather intimate dining.

Chapter 4 – Museums in Havana

A visit to the city of Havana will be akin to visiting a life size time capsule. They've got 50s style cars (sometimes older), baroque styled buildings (but you will see some 70s classic and earlier too). To help visitors understand the city's history, not to mention the country's as well, there are plenty of museums that you can visit here in Havana. We have chosen a few that will help you achieve just that – being a history buff.

National Museum of Fine Arts

- Address: Calle Trocadero e/ Zulueta y Monserrate, Havana, Cuba
- Phone: +53 7 8621643
- Date founded: February 23, 1913

This museum is located centrally at the heart of Havana's downtown area. It is also one of the city's more popular museums. It is locally known as Museo Nacional de Bellas Artes de La Habana.

Its collections belong to either the Cuban gallery or the international gallery or the universal arts. These galleries are housed in two rather impressive buildings.

Surprisingly, the Cuban gallery attracts more visitors than the international one. The Cuban gallery showcases the art produced by the artists of Havana. The collections include Spanish portraits that date back to the 17th century to the artworks of artists from the 1970s that actually lean on a more hypermodern style or genre. Some of the local artists to look out for include Wifredo Lam and René Portocarrero.

Museum of the Revolution

- Address: Calle Refugio 1 | entre Monserrate y Zulueta, Havana 10600, Cuba
- Phone: +53 7 624091
- Date established: February 23, 1913

This museum is on the same street as the National Museum of Fine Arts. This in itself is a rather impressive building. At one point it served as the country's presidential palace and was designed by Carlos Maruri a Cuban architect and Paul Belau a Belgian architect. It remained the presidential palace until the year 1959.

Living up to its namesake, the museum houses collections that have significance to the revolutionary war. It is also dedicated to the country's post war history. Some of its collections highlight the country's pre-revolutionary history as well as the war for freedom against Spain.

Some of the interesting highlights to a visit here include the Granma, the yacht that Fidel and Raul Castro, and Che Guevara sailed when they travelled from Mexico to Cuba. There are also a lot of tanks, war time vehicles, and Che Guevara's personal effects on display. They also have on display the golden telephone that was used by Fulgencio Batista.

Of course you should also take note that not everything on display here is really all about history. Part of which is only propaganda. For instance, you will find here a section of the museum which is called the Corner of the Cretins. In this section is depicted the ousted president of Cuba and the US presidents in historical tropes. Note that there are parts of this museum that may be a bit of a shock to tourists but that gives you a glimpse of the country's communist ties.

Museo del Ron Havana Club

- Avenida del Puerto 262, esq. Sol, Habana Vieja Cuba, Havana, Cuba
- +53 7 8618051 / +54 11 4413 7126
- Website: havana-club.com

Okay, so not everyone can tolerate all the artsy, historical, and intellectual stuff about Havana, not to mention Cuba too, but if you want a big break from all that and still be within the museum genre of your tour then the Havana Club Museum of Rum will be quite a pleasure.

Note however that there are English tours and Cuban tours. If you don't speak or understand Spanish, well then hop on the English tour, obviously. You will get a first-hand walk through of the Cuban way of making rum. Well, after reading the history of Cuba in book 1 of this series, you should at least know that the country is well known for this spirit. On top of that, which should be the best part of the museum tour, you get to taste free samples.

Finca La Vigia—Ernest Hemingway's Home

- Calle Obispo 153 | Carretera Central Km 12.5, Havana 10100, Cuba
- +53 7 8910809
- Historic site
- Website: www.hemingwaycuba.com/finca-la-vigia.html

Finding Ernest Hemingway's home here in Cuba will come as a surprise for many folks. A lot of the things that you will find here are references to the country's revolutionaries. Finding not only a stockpile of Hemingway's books in this city but his actual residence is a treasure trove in itself.

The author lived in Havana for two decades, which is one of the reasons why you'll find plenty of his books in second hand book stores and in markets as well. Hemingway's home is now a museum – well that's how the Cuban government put it to use after the man deeded his house to them after his suicide. The home was restored and reopened to the public in 2007.

Tourists can view the rooms, the original furniture still intact, his bookshelves, and all the other décor still untouched.

Palacio de los Capitanes Generales

- Address: Cuba Tacón, La Habana, Cuba

The name translates to Palace of the Captain Generals but it is now formally known as the Museum of the City. If you love 18th century architecture then this could come out as a treat. The building itself is fashioned in Cuban baroque style.

The place itself is quite romantic. At the center of the grounds is a courtyard and along its perimeter are several rooms that still contain canons, carriages, and other artifacts that date back to 17th century Cuba. This museum itself doesn't have a lot of exhibits. However, it is centrally located with the book seller's market right next to it and the other attractions in Havana only a stone's throw away.

Classic Car Museum

- Calle Oficios 13 e Jústiz y Obra Pía, La Habana 10100, Cuba
- +53 7 863 9942

You get a lot of the 50s vibe out of Cuba and Havana in particular. And you get a whole lot of that from the Classic Car Museum. The museum houses cars that were manufactured from 1905 to 1989. You'll basically get a tour of the country's automobile industry.

They actually have a really nice collection here. Some of the cars are pretty rare. The oldest one in the country is the museum's 1905 Cadillac. Other than the cars, you'll also find a collection of vintage Harley Davidson motorcycles.

Some of the cars you'll find here may not be that rare but they were the actual cars of celebrities and historic people of the country. For instance, you'll catch a glimpse of Fidel Castro's Ducati 900SS. You need about an hour to tour the entire museum. The admission fee is only $1, which is really cheap.

Napoleonic Museum

- Plaza de la Revolucion, Havana, Cuba
- +53 7 879 1412

It may come as a surprise to you that Cuba has a lot of French history to it. In fact, they have an entire museum that houses more than 8,000 items in its collection. Of course, we all know that Havana itself is heavily cast in Spanish culture and history but the addition of French artifacts dating from the French Revolution shows how culturally diverse the country really is.

The French artifacts include a lot of military equipment, coinage, suits, and even Napoleon's very own death mask. The museum has connections to educational institutions, namely the University of Havana. When you visit here, take advantage of the English guided tour since a lot of the items and finds here do not have any descriptions.

Chapter 5 – The Malecón

The Malecón is one of the main avenues that you will have to tread on or drive through when you visit Havana. It's the six lane avenue with a seawall on the side that protects the city from the ocean waters. This five mile stretch of an avenue is a regular place where locals and tourists hang out. It is the place where artists look for inspiration and the common man dreams of better days.

The Malecón's long stretch offers you a lot of options if you run out of places to see in Havana and you need to kill the time. It stretches from the mouth of the Almendares River to the Punta fortress. In this chapter we'll look at some of the interesting things to do and places to see in this long stretch of a seaside boulevard.

A Picturesque Walk

No doubt, there are rides on Havana including day trips that pass through the entire stretch of this wide avenue. However, you do miss out on some of the really intimate Instagram worthy shots.

5 miles is 5 miles – that should be enough a distance to give you a good jog to start up your day. If jogging is not your thing then a leisurely stroll with a camera in hand can be quite a revealing road trip. You will find a lot of parks and interesting buildings along the way. A lot of them are pretty good choices for a unique one of a kind selfie to make your friends back home jealous. Of course, the scenery of the ocean water bashing

against the seawall adds a truly dramatic effect on your pictures.

Hang Out on 23rd Street

The intersection of 23rd street and Malecón is a popular place to hang out here in Havana. It's a common gathering area for couples, teenagers, friends, and family. The National Hotel has a fountain that flows into the area provide a relaxing back drop. Everyone prefers to sit back and enjoy the cool breeze. You can even see the occasional rum being passed around among friends while local music fills the air.

Morro Lighthouse

The El Morro Castle is one of the main icons and landmarks in Havana. This is one of those must have selfie backgrounds to scream out to the world declaring that you have arrived in Havana. Don't forget to include the lighthouse when you put El Morro in the background of that one of a kind selfie.

USS Maine Monument

The USS Maine monument was erected in 1925 and it was dedicated to the victims of the attack on the USS Maine while it was in the Havana harbor in 1898. This attack triggered the United States involvement in the Cuban Revolution against Spain which eventually led to the Spanish-American War.

There used to be an eagle atop the two columns on this monument. Well, that was until 1961 when tensions spiked between the US and Cuba. The eagle on top was taken down because the people back then saw it as a symbol of imperialism. Today the monument is a place of quiet repose in memory of the brave men who fought in these wars.

José Martí Tribuna Antiimperialista

The Anti-Imperialist Platform is one of the attractions that you will come across when you hike the 5 mile length of the Malecón. It is a large square that was built right in front of the United States embassy.

Rallies, concerts, and various events are scheduled here which can become quite lively. You will also find a statue of José Martí here. He is depicted standing, holding a child in hand, protecting or shielding it from something he is pointing to in a distance.

Bar Hopping

Another reason to go hiking in the afternoon along the Malecón is the nice selection of bars that you will find along the way. A lot of these bars serve traditional Cuban cocktails along with all sorts of drinks and concoctions to your heart's content. Many of these bars have great views of the sea and some of them are overlooking the ocean. Not all bars here are regular bars – some of them are cigar bars while others are 3D cafés. The options are pretty diverse and you may end up going through several miles just to sample the best booze and other stuff in town.

Work on Your Tan or Just Fish

If you can't jog then speed walk. But if you've gotten sick of walking and you just want to sit still, then no one's going to stop you. Stretch out on a chair and work on your tan if the day is particularly sunny. Some tourists spend the entire day at the seawall just sleeping.

However, do take note that if you don't look anything like the locals then chances are there will be people who will approach you trying to sell you something. Some even just walk to you and play music. If you don't want that kind of distraction then rent a rod and reel and try your hand at fishing. You'll find that this is quite common – you can even sit down and get some chit chat with the locals as you try in hope to catch something.

Enjoy the Sunset

One of the really favorite things that people do here in the Malecón is to just sit on the sea wall in the afternoons and enjoy the view of the sunset. The sunsets here are stunning – it is perhaps one of the most picturesque things you will ever see here in Havana. Of course, some days are cloudier than others but when the weather is bright and clear, you should be ready with your camera. Set your camera's exposures, prepare your wide angle lens, and get your tripod ready.

There are plenty of things to see and do along the Malecón. You can always take some time out during your day and spend time there. You may even find a new bar nearby or just spend some quiet repose as you see the sun sink along the horizon.

Conclusion

I hope that this Havana travel guide was able to help you appreciate the wonders of this time encapsulated city. May you also capture the romance, the ideal of freedom, and the plight of the people for a better tomorrow. Most of all, may you also enjoy a wonderful Cuban vacation and frolic in the sun.

Printed in Great Britain
by Amazon